The Material Culture of the
Northern Sea Peoples in Israel

HARVARD SEMITIC MUSEUM PUBLICATIONS

Lawrence E. Stager, General Editor
Michael D. Coogan, Director of Publications

STUDIES IN
THE ARHCHAEOLOGY AND HISTORY OF THE LEVANT

Edited by
Lawrence E. Stager

1. *The Archaeology of Jordan and Beyond: Essays in Honor of James A. Sauer*, edited by Lawrence E. Stager, Joseph A. Greene, and Michael D. Coogan
2. *The House of the Father as Fact and Symbol: Patrimonialism in Ugarit and the Ancient Near East*, by J. David Schloen
3. *Canaanites, Chronologies, and Connections: The Relationship of Middle Bronze Age IIA Canaan to Middle Kingdom Egypt*, by Susan L. Cohen
4. *"Walled Up to Heaven": The Evolution of Middle Bronze Age Fortification Strategies in the Levant*, by Aaron A. Burke
5. *The Material Culture of the Northern Sea Peoples in Israel*, by Ephraim Stern
6. *Excavations at the EB IV Sites of Jebel Qaʿaqir and Beʾer Resisim*, by William G. Dever

THE MATERIAL CULTURE
OF THE NORTHERN SEA PEOPLES
IN ISRAEL

by

Ephraim Stern

Winona Lake, Indiana
EISENBRAUNS
2013

The Material Culture of the Northern Sea Peoples in Israel

by

Ephraim Stern

www.eisenbrauns.com

Library of Congress Cataloging-in-Publication Data

Stern, Ephraim, 1934- author.
  The material culture of the Northern Sea peoples in Israel / by Ephraim Stern.
      pages cm. — (Studies in the archaeology and history of the Levant ; 5)
    Includes bibliographical references and index.
    ISBN 978-1-57506-946-3 (pbk. : alk. paper)
    1. Palestine—Antiquities. 2. Material culture—Palestine. 3. Philistines—Migrations.
  4. Cyprus—Emigration and immigration. 5. Excavations (Archaeology)—Israel. 6. Dor
  (Extinct city) I. Title.
    DS121.S83 2013
    933—dc23
                                                              2013028233

In memory of Frank Moore Cross, Jr.
A teacher and a friend

CONTENTS

Preface   ix

1 Introduction   1

2 The Archaeological Evidence   5
   The Sharon and the Carmel Coast   5
   The Plain of 'Akko   18
   The Western Jezreel Valley   20

3 The Pottery   27
   Introduction   27
   Philistine Pottery Forms   31
   The Pottery of the Northern Sea Peoples   33

4 Cult Objects   43
   Introduction   43
   Clay Anthropomorphic Vessels and Figurines   43
   Bull-shaped Clay Libation Vessels   45
   Ivory Bull Plaques   43
   Gold Bull Earrings and Jewelry   47
   Wall Brackets   48
   Clay Lioness-headed Cups   50
   Clay Stands   52
   Cow Scapulae   53
   The Cylinder Seal   55

5 Burial Practices   57
   Pottery Bath   57
   Gold Plaques   57

6 Various Tools and Finds   59
   Bronze Axes and Knives   59
   Ivory Knife Handles   60
   Cypro-Minoan Inscriptions   61
   Clay Loom Weights   62

Conclusions   63

Bibliography   65

PREFACE

This monograph was written over the course of many years and is the product of my two decades of excavation at Tel Dor on the Carmel Coast, a city that Egyptian sources indicate was ruled in the eleventh century BCE by a Sikil king. Only at the end of the period during which I directed the excavation did I begin to perceive the unique material culture of the Northern Sea Peoples and to connect it with finds from the adjacent region and the north of Israel. I was greatly assisted in this by the results of the preliminary investigation of my colleague and friend, the late Avner Raban, who conducted a survey of the 'Akko Valley.

This accumulation of data, I believe, allows the characterization and classification of a new and previously unrecognized material culture, attributable to the Northern Sea Peoples, who Egyptian historical sources indicate settled in this region. Their culture, while sharing certain similarities with that of the southern Philistines, is nonetheless distinct.

This realization came before we began to hear of the finds and inscriptions reflect the contemporary existence of a large kingdom of Sea Peoples in northern Syria and southern Anatolia, beyond the Canaanite-Phoenician region between Achziv and Arvad.

In this study I have been guided by two main principles. The first is that historical sources provide the best evidence for contemporary events, in this case ones dealing with the Sikils and the Sherden, as well as biblical sources that refer to Northern Sea Peoples as "Philistines" and tell of their wars with Israel in the north of the land, in the Jezreel Valley, and Gilboa.

The second guiding principle is my belief in the concept of ethnic archaeology. I am certain that every people that settled in the Land of Israel left the mark of its own unique culture. We are able, for example, to distinguish between no less than eight different ethnic cultures existing simultaneously, side by side, during the eighth and seventh centuries BCE: Arameans, Phoenicians, Israelites, Judahites, Philistines, Ammonites, Moabites, and Edomites. In addition, there are the cultures of foreign rulers such as the Assyrians, Babylonians, and Persians, and other external influences that arrived via different routes, mostly through trade, such as Greek and Egyptian ones.

From here, I reach our topic, the culture of the Northern Sea Peoples. Indeed, it is very difficult to trace the culture of this people that lived in the north of the Land of Israel and perhaps controlled that region for a short period of a hundred years or slightly longer. Through an examination of all of the finds of the relevant strata at sites along the coast from the Yarkon northward and in the 'Akko and Jezreel valleys, it becomes clear that the Northern Sea Peoples indeed left remains that relate to nearly all aspects of their material culture, a culture that is, in part, identical or similar to that of the Philistines, and in part distinct and unique.

By material culture I do not mean only their unique pottery, but include other elements such as cult, art, burial customs, weapons, and even common everyday objects such as loom weights and similar items.

What is unique about this culture is that it is entirely of Cypriot origin, though its artifacts are locally produced, including vessels whose production had virtually ceased in Cyprus.

During the years that I worked on this topic I was assisted by several of my students and offer them my gratitude: Svetlana Matskevich, Ester Deutsch, and, in particular, Yiftah Shalev, whose assistance was essential. I also thank the many colleagues dealing with related topics who read my work and made useful comments, including Trude Dothan, Aren M. Maeir, Amihai Mazar, Lawrence E. Stager and Assaf Yasur-Landau.

For the purpose of this work I have included photographs, drawings and finds from excavations carried out by colleagues and am grateful for their permission to utilize these: M. Artzy, A. Ben-Tor, K. Cavello-Paran, T. Dothan, I. Finkelstein and D. Ussishkin, Z. Herzog, A. Mazar, P. Nahshoni, and A. Zarzecki-Peleg. The photographs from my excavation at Tel Dor were taken by Z. Radovan and G. Laron. The artifacts were drawn by Sara Halbreich. Portions of the monograph written in Hebrew were translated into English by Essa Cindorf. My sincere thanks to all the above.

I also wish to thank the editors of the Harvard Semitic Museum publications for reading this work and approving it for publication, and to Eisenbrauns for printing the volume.

Ephraim Stern

1
INTRODUCTION

The purpose of this study is to determine the unique position and chronological framework of the material culture of the Northern Sea Peoples who settled in Palestine. Up to now, the remains of this culture have, for the most part, been identified with those of the southern Philistines (T. Dothan 1982) and no genuine attempt has been made to distinguish between the two and to establish the similarities and the diferences existing between the Northern Sea Peoples and the Philistines. In this study I will attempt—based on the evidence uncovered during my many years of excavation at Tel Dor, the capital of the Sikils—to classify the stratigraphic remains and material culture of the Sikils and draw conclusions concerning them.

I have limited the area examined to the coast of Palestine from the Yarkon River northward, including the Plain of 'Akko and the western Jezreel Valley on the Megiddo-Afula line, since these areas produced extensive remains of the presence of tribes of Sea Peoples and evidence of their activities. However, that is not to say that they did not penetrate into other areas as well.

I will preface my discussion by presenting my three main conclusions:

1. In the area examined it is possible to distinguish the material culture characteristic of the Northern Sea Peoples which exhibits elements that are partly identical with and partly unlike those of the Philistines.
2. The source of this culture is derived almost in its entirety from Cyprus but the great majority of the finds were manufactured in Palestine by local Sea Peoples and not imported through trade with Cyprus.
3. The time range of this culture is actualy of briefer duration than that of the Philistines and apparently did not last much longer than one hundred and thirty years, from the end of the twelfth century, or perhaps a little later, to the end of the eleventh century, when it was displaced in its entirety by the local Israelite one. This short duration stands in contrast to the historical records which mention the Sikils already a century earlier. Perheps the reason is that thier impact on the local material culture was felt only somewhat later.

This study and my analysis of the finds are based on the work of Trude Dothan, who pioneered the identification of all aspects of the Philistine culture, and on that of my colleagues Amihai Mazar, Larry Stager and Aren Maeir, who conducted excavations at Tell Qasile,

Ashkelon, and Gath. I also wish to express my gratitude to the late Avner Raban who was the trailblazer in the identification of the Northern Sea Peoples.

Historical records concerning the settlement of Sea Peoples in northern Palestine are rare. There are no biblical references to the Sikils, Sherden, or Denyen or to their role in the settlement history of this region. The Bible mentions only the Philistines, whose area of settlement extended along the southern coast up to the Yarkon River where their northern limit is marked by their settlements at Aphek, Tell Qasile, Tel Gerisa, and Jaffa (Fig. 1). Historical references to the Sikils and other Sea Peoples are in fact confined to extrabiblical sources, principally those from Egypt. Ramesses III, who ejected the Sea Peoples from Egypt in c. 1180 BCE, recorded that he "destroyed" three of them: The Denyen, the Sikils, and the Philistines. An Ugaritic text, which is earlier, mentions the Sikils as pirates who live on their ships (Lehmann 1979: RS 34.129, 20.238; Stager 1995: 337).

Most of our information about these tribes, however, is derived from two slightly later Egyptian documents (Dietrich and Loretz 1978). The first is the Onomasticon of Amenope dating to the late twelfth or early eleventh century BCE that consists of a list of names, among which appear "Ashkelon, Ashdod, Gaza, . . . Sherden, Sikils, and Philistia." The text thus refers to three coastal Philistine cities (Ashkelon, Ashdod, and Gaza) and three tribes of Sea Peoples (Sherden, Sikils, and Philistines) and it is possible that both the Sikils and the Sherden ruled parts of the northern and central Palestinian coast (Gardiner 1947).

The second and more detailed document, the "Tale of Wenamun" (Fig. 1) from el-Hibeh in middle Egypt, dates to the early Twenty-first Dynasty, in the first half of the eleventh century BCE (Wilson 1955; Goedicke 1975; Nibbi 1985; Scheepers 1991; Schipper 2005; King 2009). It contains the only reference to the Sikil settlement at Dor and is probably the most important document for the history of Palestine during the "dark age" of the eleventh century BCE. The author, Wenamun, was a priest in the temple of Amon at Karnak who was sent to purchase cedar wood for the sacred barge. Wenamun relates: "I reached Dor, a town of the Sikils, and Beder, its prince, had fifty loaves of bread, one jug of wine, and one leg of beef brought to me" (Wilson 1955:26). Later in the story, he tells how one of his ship's crewmen made off with a large quantity of his gold and silver, leaving Wenamun penniless. Wenamun appealed to the governor of Dor to capture the thief and restore his goods. As that potentate was not particularly eager to fulfill this request, Wenamun despaired of any help from the people of Dor and took refuge first at Tyre, then later at Byblos. After further adventures in Byblos, Wenamun realized that Beder's men were in pursuit: "And I went to the shore of the sea to the place where the timber was lying and I spied eleven ships belonging to the Sikils coming in from the sea in order to say: 'Arrest him! don't let a ship of his go to the land of Egypt.' " (Wilson 1955:28).

The Tale of Wenamun, which may be based on an official report,[1] makes it clear that the Sikils were settled at Dor and that they operated a large fleet from the harbor. Apart from Beder, the story mentions three other rulers, whose names may belong to the Sea Peoples, although some scholars think that they were Egyptians. One of them, Weret, was probably the ruler of Ashkelon. (cf. Maeir et al. 2008). He had a trading treaty with the powerful maritime city of Tyre. The two others may have been the governors of Ashdod and Gaza.

This important document presents a unique picture of the autonomous coastal cities in the eleventh century BCE. Some were ruled by the Sea Peoples and others by Phoenicians. They maintained commercial ties with one another and evidently controlled the Palestinian and Phoenician coast independently of Egypt (Wilson 1955; B. Mazar 1974; Goedicke 1975; Nibbi 1985; Bietak 1993; Moers 1995; Bains 1999; O'Connor 2000; Egberts 2001, but see also Sass 2002; and recently King 2009 and bibliography there).

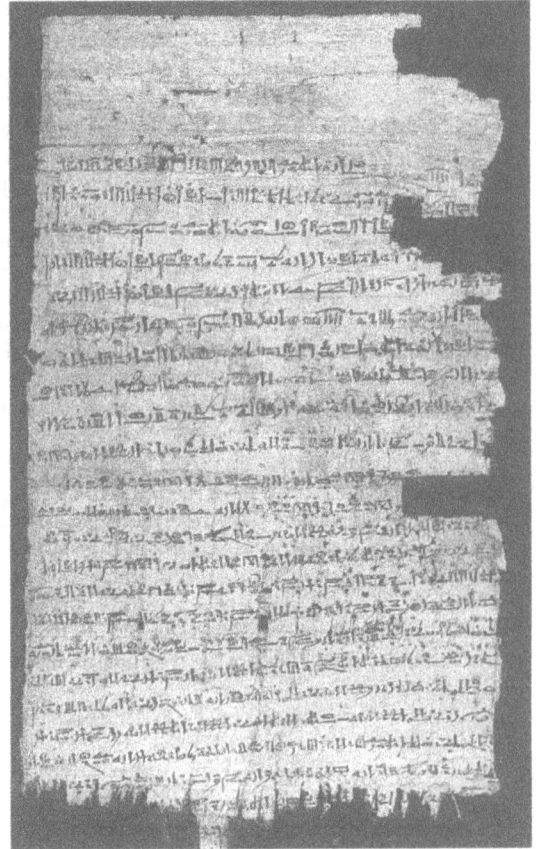

Figure 1. The papyrus of Wenamun.

[1] In the past the Wenamun text was considered a literary reworking of an administrative document. The scholar responsible for a change in this approach was J. Černy (1952) who claimed that the text was "almost certainly the original report." His arguments were roughly as follows: Literary texts were written in columns across the width of the papyrus scroll and the scribe held the parchment open along its width. When writing administrative documents, the scribe held the rolled-up scroll facing him, along its length and wrote in lines perpendicular to the width. When he finished a document, he cut the scroll along the actual length of the text. The Wenamun scroll was therefore made up of only two pages, with the first one consisting of 59 lines and the second holds 83 lines.

H. Goedicke, who made a thorough study of the Wenamun document (1975), agreed with Cerny that the scroll was an administrative document (and not a fictional narrative) but he claimed that the papyrus was not an original document as proposed by Cerny but a copy. In his opinion, however, the value of the copy was equal to that of the original! Why did he consider the papyrus a copy and not the original?

The writing flows and is not that of someone who is composing a document and stopping from time to time to collect his thoughts and consider the continuation. In the first part of the papyrus some of the sentences are written in red for emphasis, as in formal copies of documents, and not drafts. In the second part, something is deleted in line 63 causing a break in the subject—it is possible that the copier's attention was momentarily diverted. The text ends abruptly despite the fact that there was still room on the papyrus (as many as four lines), as if someone decided that the continuation (concerning Wenamun's tribulations in Alashiya and his return to Egypt) are of no interest to him. In the remaining space is written the word "copy" (ḥt).

The original was apparently composed by Wenamun immediately on his return to Egypt: He departed from Egypt in the twenty-third regnal year of Ramesses XI (1114–1087 BCE) and returned two years later. The copy we possess, however, is apparently from a later date. Already in 1909, G. Moeller dated the papyrus on paleographical grounds to the 22nd dynasty, i.e., about 150 years later than the composition of the original document (Moller 1909). Goedicke accepts this view which he corroborates with the following evidence: The word ht ("copy") is documented for the first time during the 22nd dynasty; the verso of the papyrus contains two lines whose script can be dated on paleographic grounds to the 22nd dynasty; and finally, the papyrus was discovered at el-Hibeh, which was built and flourished during the 21st–22nd dynasties.

In 2002 B. Sass returned to the earlier theory that the Wenamun text was not a later copy of an earlier document, but a later original text from the time of Pharaoh Shishak (925 BCE), founder of the 22nd dynasty. Sass believes it represented a document composed by Shishak as propaganda against the previous (21st) dynasty. This view, however, seems unreasonable and has been justly challenged by S. Aḥituv, who stated in a letter to me: "The writer has exact information about the coast, about Dor and Byblos. He knows the name and origin of the king of Dor and also that the king of Byblos is called Zakar-Baal and, in fact, we possess two arrows of the latter, or of someone from his dynasty, which are inscribed: 'An arrow of Zakar-Baal, King of the Amurru.'"

The theory that the story was propaganda disseminated by Shishak against the previous dynasty to emphasize its weakness seems far-fetched. This would assume that the text was written by a very sophisticated writer and was intended for an audience of the most discriminating tastes and refined literary and political perception. In actual fact, the tale is not the height of literary sensitivity, nor does it contain a single word against the previous dynasty (21st). It never mentions Ramasses XI, and Smendes and his wife and Herihor are referred to without any criticism. Was the text censored in any way? Some derogatory texts do exist. Aḥituv gives examples of Thutmose III's criticism of Hat-sheptsut and the motif of chaos in contrast to the order brought about by a new king (as the situation prior to the accession of Set-Nakht, founder of the 20th dynasty, is described in the Papyrus Anastasi I), but there is nothing similar here. It should also be recalled—according to Aḥituv—that Shishak did not overthrow the preceding dynasty; on the contrary, he was connected with it through family ties and the transition was a peaceful one (and cf. recently: King 2009).

2
THE ARCHAEOLOGICAL EVIDENCE

THE SHARON AND THE CARMEL COAST

The data contained in the above-mentioned documents as well as the biblical sources indicate that after the destruction of the Canaanite world, Philistines had settled in southern Palestine; the Bible, the Egyptian sources, and the archaeological evidence all provide considerable information about Philistine domination and settlement of this area and about their five great cities. As was stated above, their northern border was at the Yarkon River, where the remains of several flourishing Sea Peoples' cities were uncovered: The first, Tel Aphek, was excavated by M. Kochavi and published by Gadot and Yadin (Beck and Kochavi 1993; Gadot 2006; Gadot and Yadin 2009:300–314); others include Tell Qasile with its buildings and temples, discovered by B. and A. Mazar (Mazar 1980; 1985a); Tel Gerisa, excavated by Z. Herzog (Herzog 1993); Jaffa, excavated by J. and H. Kaplan (Kaplan and Ritter-Kaplan 1993); and perhaps also Azor excavated by M. Dothan (Stern 1993:128-129; Ben-Shlomo 2008b). It now seems to the present writer that in these border towns both the Philistines and the Northern Sea Peoples lived together. The Sikils probably occupied the Sharon, and the Sherden perhaps an area farther north, in the Plain of 'Akko and its surroundings (see below).

Excavations have indeed confirmed these suppositions. Finds that the present writer ascribed to the Sikils have been discovered at Tel Ḥefer, Tel Zeror, Tel Dor, and other sites along the coast (and see below), while at Tel 'Akko and nearby Tell Keisan, excavations uncovered pottery attributed by the excavators of these two sites to the Sherden (M. Dothan 1986; 1989; Singer 1988; Raban 1991; Stern 2000b and B. Mazar 1974). I shall demonstrate in the following detailed discussions that this peculiar material culture evidently belonged to the Northern Sea Peoples rather than the Philistines.

To understand the magnitude of the revolution that took place on the northern coast of Palestine from the Yarkon northward to the Plain of 'Akko—the subject of our discussion—we must first examine settlements in the area preceding this transformation, settlements which belonged to the Canaanites who had occupied this area over the course of many centuries. In some half-dozen sites excavated in this part of the coast, an identical picture was observed by the excavators at each of the sites; these will be discussed here from south to north (Fig. 2).

All the sites on the Canaanite coast of the Ḥefer Valley, in the Sharon, and on the Carmel coast—without exception—were laid waste at the end of the thirteenth century BCE in a total destruction that put an end to Canaanite culture and Egyptian domination. This destruction has been attributed by the excavators of all the settlements in these areas to the Sea Peoples (Gadot 2008, Paley and Porath 1993; Kochavi 1993; Herzog, Rapp, and Negbi 1989; Stern 1978; Stern 2000; Artzy 1993; Elgavish 1994; M, Dothan 1955; 1986; Ben-Tor, Bonfil, and Zuckerman 2003; Ben-Tor, Zarzecki-Peleg, and Cohen-Anidjar 2005).

Following this destruction, four groups of settlements can be distinguished. The first comprises Late Bronze Age settlements which were destroyed and never rebuilt. The most prominent example in this group is Tel Nami (Artzy 1993; 1995). The second group consists of sites that were rebuilt after a gap extending through the entire Iron Age I. These settlements recovered only in the period of the monarchy; the entire period of the Sea Peoples' occupation bypassed them. Examples include Tel Michal (Strata XV–XIV; Herzog, Rapp, and Negbi 1989) and Tel Mevorakh (Strata IX–VIII; Stern 1978:76).

The third group consists of settlements which were rebuilt on their ruins and contain remains associated with the settlement of the Sea Peoples in the area: Tel Ḥefer (Paley and Porath 1993:612), Tel Zeror (Kochavi 1993), and Tel Dor. Although the Bronze Age stratum of destruction at the last site has not yet been reached, the new Sikil city that replaced it extended over an area five times the conjectured size of the last Canaanite city (Stern 2000a:85–101, 345–353). Shiqmona may perhaps be another example; at this site the Canaanite Stratum 16 was leveled and Strata 15–13 of the Iron Age I were constructed above it (Elgavish 1994).

A fourth separate group represents new settlements established by the Sea Peoples on sites not previously occupied, of which Tell Qasile is the most prominent example (A. Mazar 1980; 1985a). As noted above Qasile was established in our opinion as a common settlement of both Philistines and Northern Sea Peoples.

The settlements in the Plain of 'Akko—Tell Abu Hawam, 'Akko, and Tell Keisan—also suffered destruction. At these three sites, occupation was renewed in the Iron Age I, apparently after a gap, and the new settlements can be attributed to the Sea Peoples. The same situation

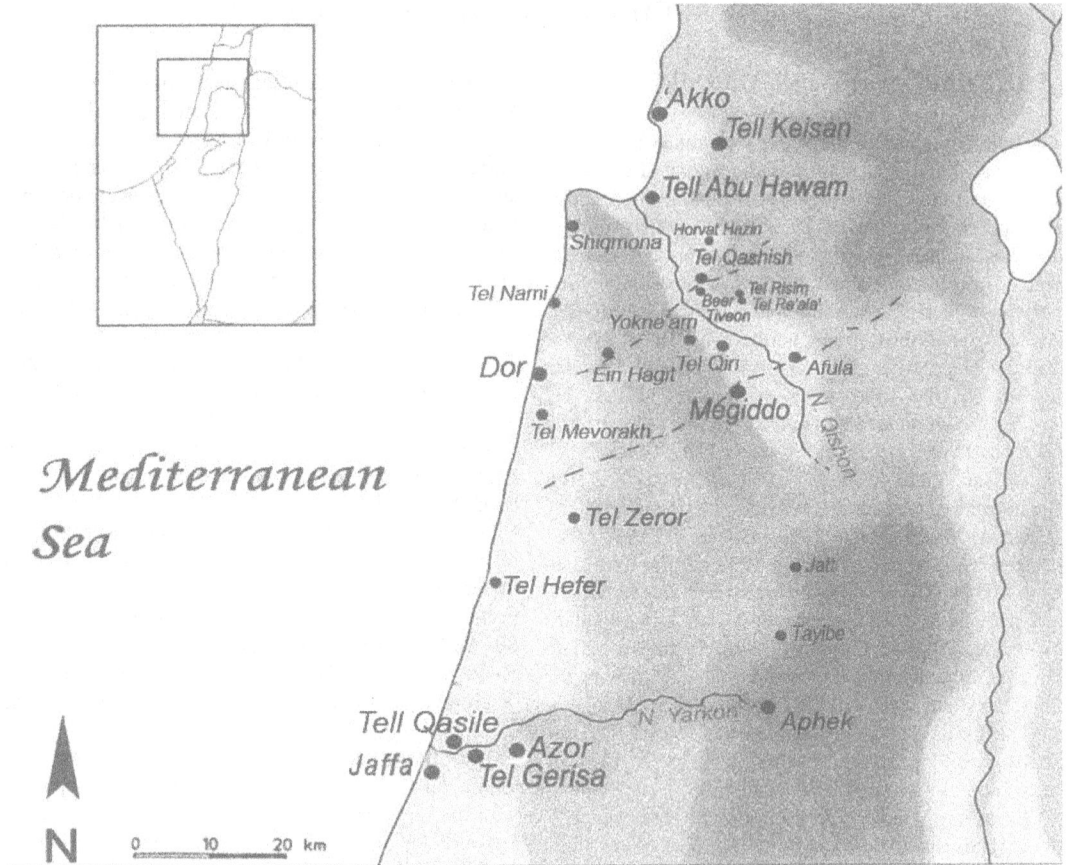

Figure 2. Map of Iron Age I sites in northern Israel containing remains of the Sea Peoples.

can be found in the western Jezreel Valley, at Megiddo, Tel Qiri, Tel Qashish, Afula, and others. All these sites will be discussed in detail below. According to the biblical testimony the Jezreel Valley was—during the days of Saul—under Philistine (i.e., Sea Peoples) rule: "The Philistines mustered and they marched to Shunem and encamped" (1 Samuel 28:4; see also 1 Samuel 29:1 and 11). Later comes the story of the last stand of Saul on Mount Gilboa and the presenting of his body on the walls of Beth-Shean. All this has been summed up by B. Halpern thus: "The Philistines, after all, were projecting their influence up the coast and across the Jezreel Valley" (Halpern 2009:159).

Whereas the settlement of the Northern Sea Peoples—based on the historical sources mentioned above—is associated with the central and northern coastal areas—the Philistines up to the Yarkon; the Sikils to the north of the Yarkon on the coast of the Hefer Valley, in the Sharon, and on the Carmel; and the Sherden beyond them in the north (in the Plain of 'Akko). The question of their possible control of areas farther inland, especially in the eastern Jezreel Valley and Beth-Shean, can be determined only on the basis of the archaeological evidence (A. Mazar 1993).

Consequently, we have focused here—for reasons of brevity—on a very restricted area in the hinterland: The western Jezreel Valley (up to the Megiddo–Afula line), so as not to belabor the subject needlessly and also because of the unambiguous nature of the material culture of this area as compared with the others.

The "Phoenician" coast from 'Akko northward is also not included in this study, since in our opinion, it was almost immediately resettled (after its destruction at the end of the thirteenth century) by Canaanites-Phoenicians (Stern 1990; 1991) and we assume it was never included in the area occupied by "our" Sea Peoples (but in this matter, see Coubet 1992, and recently also Gilboa 2001b; 2005).

At the same time it is clearly evident that the material culture influences of these Sea Peoples is now strongly attested in the Hattai region, farther north and beyond the Phoenician area (Singer 2012). This is shown by the results of the recent excavations in that area, results summarized by one of the excavators, T. P. Harrison, as: "Somewhat unexpectedly, however, the early Iron Age levels at Ta'yinat have also revealed a material culture signature that betrays an intrusive Aegean influence, if not direct evidence of the presence of foreign settlers." He adds: "This early Iron Age polity also exhibits strong Aegean cultural associations, both in its material culture, and now also epigraphically" (Harrison 2009: 181; cf. Janeway 2006-2007). These conclusions hold in my mind also for many other sites in this region. Other scholars disagree (e.g., Sherratt 1998; Gilboa 1999b; Gilboa 2009; Gilboa and Sharon 2003; Gilboa, Sharon, and Zorn 2004).

The situation is similar in the Beth-Shean Valley, and perhaps also in the northern Jordan Valley, areas that may have been briefly, in whole or in part, within the area of settlement or influence of the Sea Peoples (see also the biblical account of the war between Saul and the "Philistines" on Mount Gilboa [1 Samuel 31], and also Yadin 1968; Negbi 1991; Tubb 1988; 2000; Mazar 1993; 1994).

Despite our assumption that extensive areas on the northern coast and in the Plain of 'Akko and the Jezreel Valley were occupied by the Sea Peoples, we have chosen to begin our survey of the areas settled by the Northern Sea Peoples and the discussion of their characteristic remains at *Tel Dor* (Fig. 3), both because it is the only northern settlement for which there is documentary evidence of rule by a Sikil king (see above and also Ben Dov 1976) and according to the Bible (1 Kings 4:11), it served after that as Solomon's fourth district capital. From these sources we can thus deduce dates for the beginning and end of Sikil rule at the site.

A second reason is purely subjective: For two decades the present writer directed large-scale excavations at Tel Dor and personally witnessed the unearthing of a large amount of varied remains from the period of the Sikil rule of the city and the discovery of strata associated with the Sea Peoples in different parts of the mound.

Figure 3. Tel Dor, aerial photo, looking northwest.

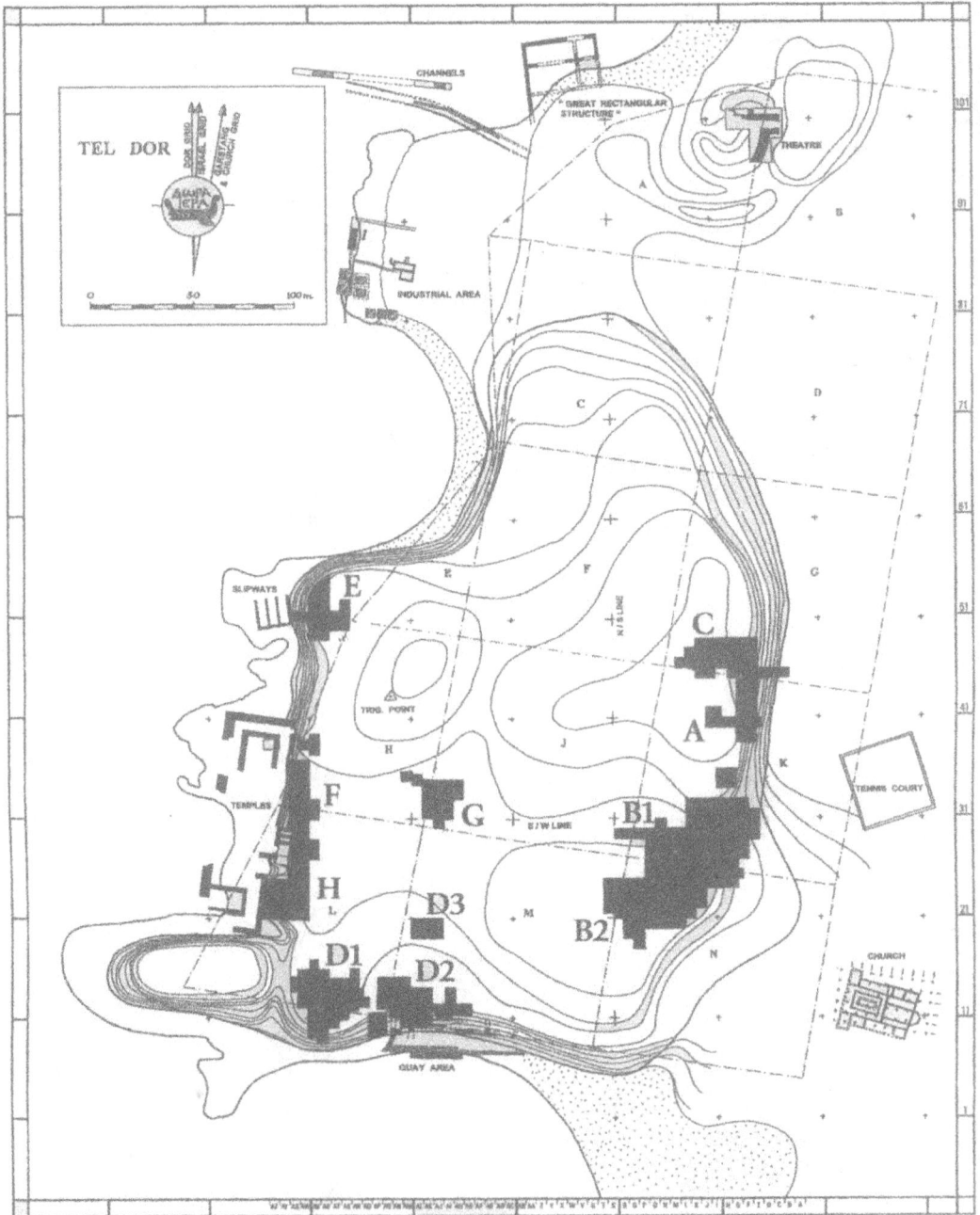

Figure 4. Tel Dor excavation areas.

Figure 5. Dor: Cypriot and local imitation of "pictorial pottery style" vessels.

Although the overall excavated area of these strata was relatively limited, a pottery assemblage was uncovered which is—in my opinion—peculiar to the Sikils. Similar finds were also made at 'Akko, Tell Keisan, Megiddo, Yokne'am and other sites along the western part of the Jezreel Valley up to the modern city of Afula. This ceramic group, which is unique to the Northern Sea Peoples, will be discussed below.

The first excavation area associated with the Sikils at Dor was Area B1 on the eastern side of the mound (Stern 1991; 2000a:85–101, 345–353, and see Fig. 4), where a thick destruction layer (local Stratum 12) was reached. It contained traces of a fierce conflagration that had oxidized the mud bricks and pulverized the limestone used in the buildings, leaving great expanses of ash and charcoal. Since this stratum of destruction was sealed by floors (local Stratum 11), on which pottery from the late eleventh century BCE was found, some of which belonged to the rare Cypriot "pictorial pottery style," both imported and locally imitated (Iacovou 1992; 1994, here Fig. 5), it served to date the remains of the earlier Sikil city.

The layer was about 2 m. thick and the floor below it consisted of thick plaster. We excavated only limited areas of this stratum, including parts of two rooms separated by an extremely thick wall. The total area excavated here is a narrow strip about 10 m. long and less than 10 m. wide.

The building abuts the eastern city wall, a large and strongly built structure with a 3 m. high base of very large stones. The inner side of the base is straight and the outer was diagonal; a structure of which two rooms were excavated was built against it. On the outer eastern side a sloping wall, over 2 m. wide at the bottom and narrowing toward the top, supported a strong wall made of flat, square mud-bricks preserved to a height of about 50 cm. Sand banked against the outer city wall protected its foundations, making Dor one of the strongest contemporary fortified cities discovered in Palestine

(Stern 2000a:88–93; Matskevich 2003; here Figs. 9-10).

Other probe shafts were dug on the western side of the mound in Areas F and E. In Area F, on the seashore, was found what seemed to be the same thick destruction layer caused by a conflagration that had charred the bricks and limestone, but a clear-cut floor level was not reached at this spot. A similar feature was observed in Area E, also located on the seashore on the western side of the mound, where the remains of two rooms destroyed in the great conflagration were uncovered.

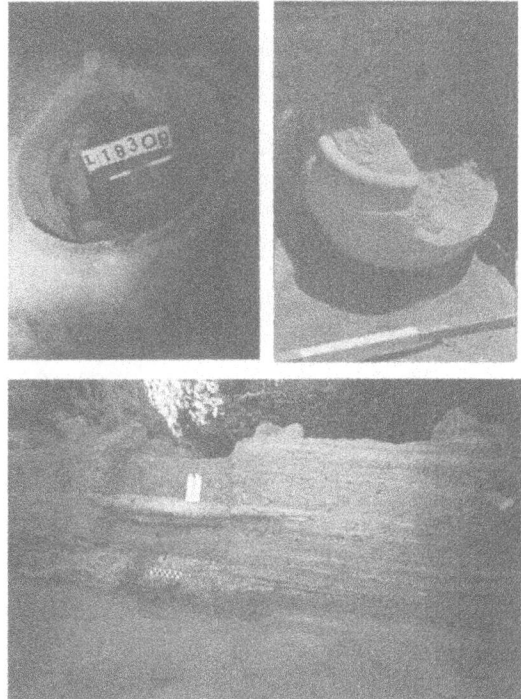

Figure 6. Dor: Remains of vessels and the ash of the copper industry in Area G.

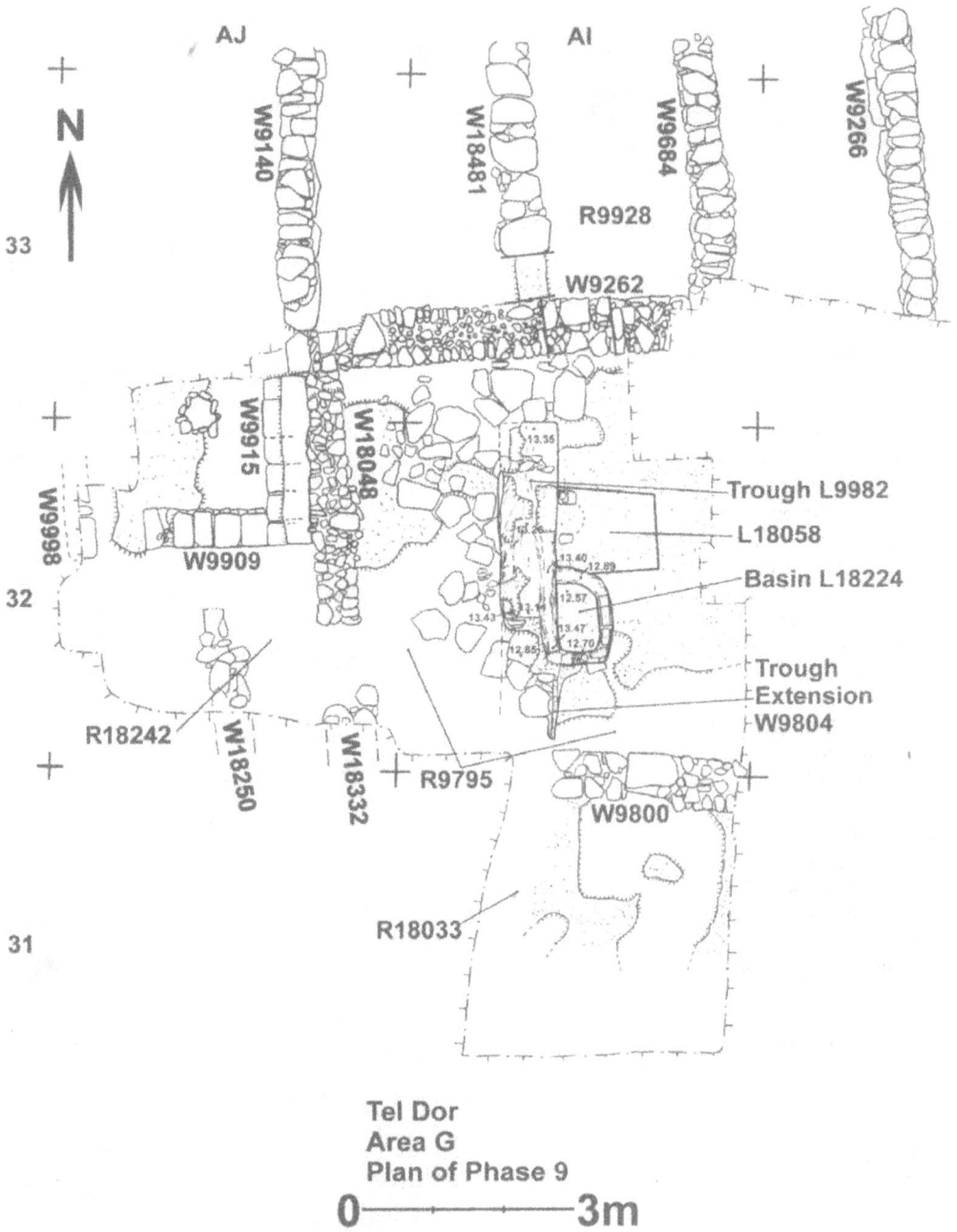

Figure 7. Dor: Area G, Phase 9: Plan of the building.

Already at this stage of the excavations, after taking into account the distance between Areas B1 and E-F on the eastern and western edges of the mound, I came to the conclusion that the city of this period occupied the entire area of the mound, and was almost five times larger than the now-estimated area of the previous Late Bronze Age town.

During the 1990s, the Sikil city was examined in two other areas: Area G in the center of the mound, and Area D2 on the southern side. Contrary to the picture revealed in Area B1, in these two areas (in which larger sections were dug), two phases of the Sikil settlement were exposed (Phases 10–9 in Area G and Phases 13–12 in Area D2), indicating that it was of much longer duration than I previously had thought.

Of the Sikil phases in Area G, the lower ones contained thick accumulations of a waste of bronze industrial ash (more than a meter high), scant building remains, and traces of a secondary metallurgical (bronze) industry, whose exact nature could not be ascertained, but which yielded fragments of bellows, crucibles, and various other artifacts as well as chunks of copper (Fig. 6). A few bronze tools, including a knife and a pick, were also uncovered (Fig. 59).

Although no clear indications of iron-working were found here, evidence of its existence may be attested by the discovery of the bone handle of a knife in the shape typical of the Sea Peoples in one of the Sikil phases (9) and another knife in Area D2 (see below). A similar complete knife (with handle and blade), uncovered in a Philistine sanctuary at Ekron, was equipped with an iron blade (Dothan and Gitin 1990:33; see here Fig. 62:1).

Phase 9 in Area G (Fig. 7), the upper Sikil phase, was first encountered on the western side of the area. In this phase, in a domestic cult room which included an offering bench attached to a wall, were found about a dozen pottery vessels, mostly small offering bowls, and two other cult vessels typical of the Sea Peoples, which will be discussed below.

On the southern side of Area G, beneath a massive burnt layer, were uncovered the remains of a large structure, whose complete plan and dimensions are outside the excavated area. This building probably belonged to a high-ranking official (cf. plan, and Zorn 2009:268*; fig. 1; here Fig. 7). We excavated only a section of this structure, including a kitchen and a store room south of the kitchen. In the center of the kitchen stood a long narrow installation made of unfired clay, at least 5 m. long, 1 m. high and 0.8 m. wide, which may have served for grinding or for preparing dough (cf. Zorn 2009 and

Fig. 8). The latter possibility is suggested by the discovery of a large basalt upper grinding stone of a previously unknown type that may have been used for grinding grain, as well as parts as other basalt vessels (cf. Zorn 2009:269*, Fig. 2).

Figure 8. Dor: Area G, Phase 9: The clay installation (top); Boetian clay model showing women kneading dough at communal trough (bottom).

Adjoining this room to the south was another store-room full of clay vessels; a number of smaller rooms to its west also contained pottery vessels and other artifacts. On the floor, in a thick ash layer, was found the handle of the above-mentioned iron knife (Fig. 62:2).

J. R. Zorn, who recently dealt in detail with this installation (Zorn 2009:267*-280*), designates it as a trough and brings many examples from all over the Near East, and thinks that it was originated there. The present writer, however, tends to compare it, being as yet a unique find in the country, to the Aegean types, as suggested by A. Stewart during the excavation (Fig. 8).

Around the clay installation and in the surrounding rooms we found a large and unusual assemblage of pottery consisting of a number of characteristic types, two local, two of Aegean origin and one Egyptian:

1. Local coastal ware, mainly jars of the latest type of "Canaanite commercial jar." Identical jars were also found in the Sikil stratum of Area B1.

2. Ordinary local collared-rim jars of a late type.

3. Sea Peoples' pottery, including some common bichrome "Philistine" ware. The bulk of this pottery, however, was of the unique monochrome type widespread in the northern Palestinian coastal plain, the western Galilee, and the western Jezreel Valley. All of this pottery is decorated with classic "Philistine" painted patterns, but in monochrome rather than the usual bichrome. This group includes kraters, bell-shaped bowls, strainer-spouted jugs, *bilbil*-shaped jugs, pyxides, flasks, and stirrup vases, all of them imitating vessels of Cypriot origin, as well as many local types, such as jars and jugs bearing the typical red-purple and sometimes also the black monochrome painted decoration.

4. Fragments of huge pithoi with relief decorations (also found in Areas B1 and D1), also of Cypriot origin.

5. Finally, a group of about eight Egyptian storage jars that were produced in the Egyptian Delta region.

The concentration of so great a variety of characteristic types in the same small floor area not only attests to the existence of extensive maritime trade (as reflected in the Wenamun tale; cf. also Stern 1993b and Master 2009), but also provides a rare chronological "window of opportunity" for these vessels: In my opinion, they could have occurred in a cluster at only one specific time in history, the eleventh century BCE.

The last area in which we penetrated into Sikil strata is Area D2 on the south side of the mound, facing the Sea Peoples' main harbor (Raban 1987; 1988).

Here, during the last two seasons of excavations directed by the writer, beneath a huge brick building we unearthed a structure (local Phases 13–12) that consisted of at least two phases. This was a monumental structure of which only well-built stone foundations were preserved to floor level. The building was constructed on bedrock and was the lowest structure on the site (like the Sikil settlement in Area B1). We excavated only the southern end of the building, facing the bay. The solid southern wall of the building formed the city's outer wall (like the eastern wall of Phase 12 in Area B1). Inside the wall we cleared a row of rooms, on the floors of which lay another group of Sea Peoples' pottery, as well as the bone handle of an iron knife similar to the one from Area G. The western end of this wall abutted the earlier wall that surrounded the town's acropolis. Above this phase no signs of a destruction level were preserved, unlike other areas, probably because the intensive construction work above it (namely, the massive foundations of the solid "brick structure"; see further below) completely erased this level. Here too, prior to the construction of this first building phase, some sort of metallurgical activity may have taken place—as was attested by the discovery of a thick layer of industrial ash beneath the building and outside it.

In addition to the Sea Peoples' pottery and the bone handle of the iron knife (see below and Fig. 62:2), another typical Sea Peoples' cult vessel was discovered—an anthropomorphic juglet depicting a human figure with slanted, coffee-bean shaped eyes (see below and Fig. 42:1).

In summary, the examination of the Sikil remains from all the excavated areas at Dor (mainly Areas B1, G and D2) reveals that they were engaged in industrial activities involving metal processing. Already during their initial occupation of the site, their building activities were intensive, and included the construction of a solid city wall to enclose the significantly larger city. It was interesting to note that, with the arrival of the Sikils, the area of the walled city expanded to five times its extent in the Bronze Age. According to A. Raban, who conducted underwater investigations around the mound, the southern harbor, which became the city's main harbor from this time onward, was also first constructed in this period. This picture agrees fully with the description of the city presented in the Wenamun tale and is far from being a "dark-age" settlement. The excavation of the Sikil strata at Dor also threw light on aspects of the material culture unique to the Northern Sea Peoples, discussed in detail below.

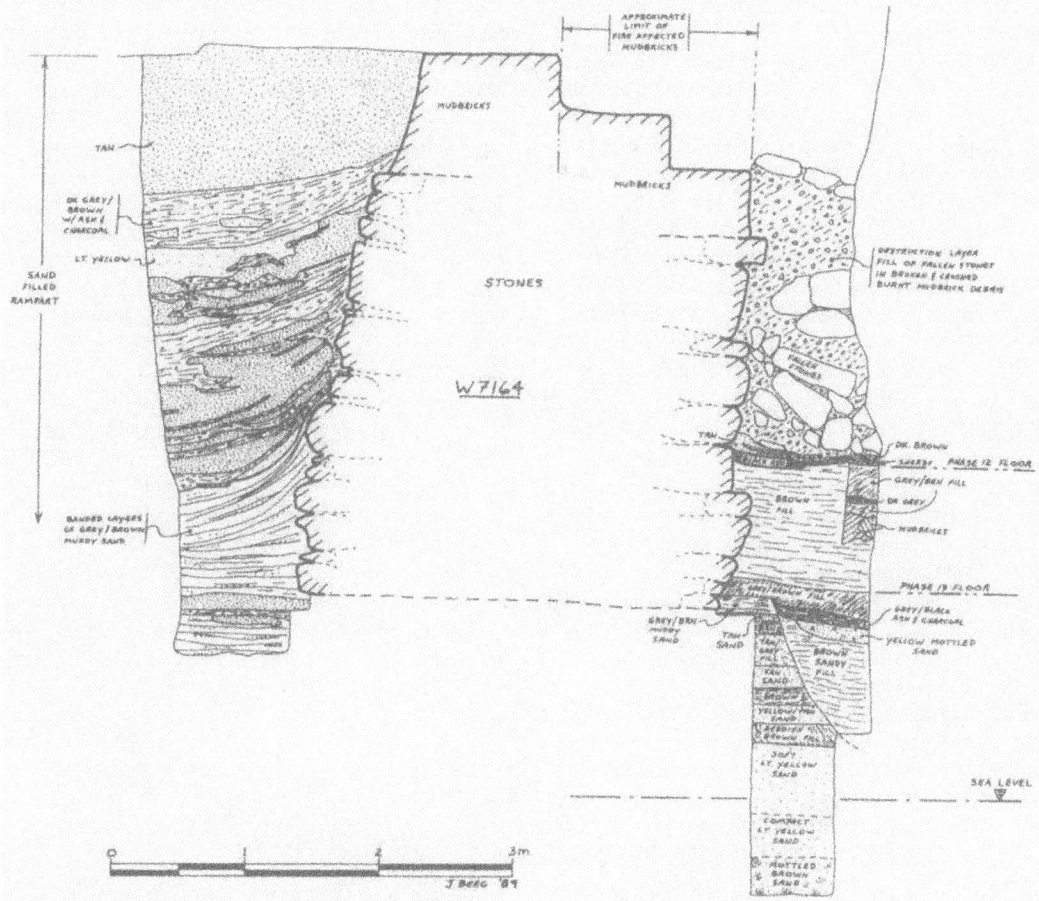

Figure 9. Dor: Section of city wall in Stratum 12, Area B1 with the massive stone foundations and the earthen embarkment, facing south.

Regarding Aegean influence on the architecture at Dor, it should be noted that because of the limited excavated area only two major Aegean influences could be identified:

1. The Cyclopean foundation of the wall on the east side (Area B1, phase 12), with straight inner face and diagonal outer face–a building type not previously encountered in Palestine (Figs. 9-10)–whose continuation apparently formed the southern outer wall of the structure in Stratum 13 in area D2 the south (the outer wall facing the sea beneath the sea-wall).

2. The trough-shaped clay installation in Phase 9, Area G (Fig. 8) that is without parallel in the local architecture but was well known in the Greek world (see above, and cf. Stern 2000a: 348, Fig. 247).

Of the rest of the Iron Age I settlement at Dor that followed this massive destruction—Phases 11–9 in Area B1, Phases 8–7 in Area G and Phases 11–9 in Area D2—only small sections of the first two areas were excavated. In Area D2, on the other hand, a monumental, exceptionally well-preserved brick building was uncovered with its west wall abutting the acropolis wall, whose foundations belonged to a much earlier date. On the south side of the building, which faced the bay and harbor, a massive stone wall (the "seawall") was added, which was also preserved to a great height and protected the city on this side (Fig. 11).

The finds from the above phases, whose maximum time span is 1050–980 BCE, are of a mixed character, with some continuing the earlier Sea Peoples' tradition and others reflecting even earlier local traditions. A new element that makes its first appearance here is the Phoenician bichrome ware; a number of sherds of a rare early type of this pottery were uncovered.

In the past, I have maintained that the massive destruction of Dor occurred as a result of the Phoenician conquest and expansion southward from the part of the coast of Phoenicia still occupied by them (Stern 2000: 101–104). Although I stand firm on this opinion—and will do so until it is proved otherwise—I now believe that I exaggerated the "Phoenicianization" of Dor after the city's destruction and up to the time of the Israelite conquest. There is no doubt that the picture is somewhat more complex. As we noted above, in these phases the city's population consisted of three different ethnic elements: the "old" Canaanites, the Sikils, and the "new" Phoenicians, but which of these elements ruled Dor after Beder, the Sikil king, and the other settlements at that time cannot be known. It is even possible that a different dynasty ruled each settlement.

It has, furthermore, now become evident that the phenomenon of rebuilding by a population made up of these three components was in fact not unique to Dor: The same scenario was repeated at Tell Qasile in the transition from Stratum XI to X, at Tell Keisan from 9c to 9a–b, at Afula from IIIB to IIIA, and especially at Megiddo in the transition from VIB to VIA. It can be assumed—although sufficient evidence is lacking—that the same situation existed at Yokne'am (XVIII–XVII) and Tel Qiri (IX–VIII) (and see charts).

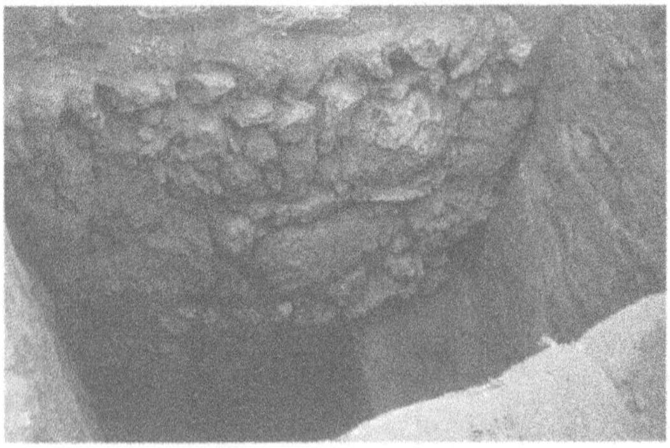

Figure 11. Dor: The 'Sea Wall.'

Figure 10. Dor: The Cyclopean wall foundations. Note the brick work above it.

	Qasile	Gerisa	Jaffa	Aphek	Hefer	Zeror	Dor (B1)	Dor (G LB)	Dor (D2)	Ein Hagit	Shikmona	Michal	Mevorakh
1200		LB	LB	LB	A7	Late LB	B1	G / LB	D2		16	XV	IX
1150 (1130)	XII												
1100	XI	"Philistine Settlement"					13-12	10 / 9	13-12	Sea People Rural Settlement	15 / 14 / 13		
1050	X		IIIB	X-10 / X-9	A6 / A5	Sea People Citadel and Cemetery	11-9	8-7	11-9				
980	IX / VIII			X-8	A4	Stone Structures	8	6 b-a	8 c-b		12	XIV / XIII	VIII / VII

Date	Tell Abu Hawam	'Akko	Keisan	Megiddo	Yokne'am	Qiri	Qashish	Afula
1200	Early Vc	LB	12 – 13	VIIB	XIX	IX	V	IV
1150 (1130)		New Population + "Shardinian" Pottery		VIIA Egyptian or Canaanite				
1100			11-9c	VIB	XVIII		IV	III B
1050	Late Vc / IV 1-2 / IV 3-4	Few Finds	9 a-b	VIA	XVII	VIII		
980	IV 5 – / III Early		8c	VC? / VB / VA-IVB	XVI - XIV	VII	III B	III A

At the same time, however, it should be emphasized that because of the limited area excavated at Dor, a full picture of the material culture of the Northern Sea Peoples (at present, the Sikil culture cannot be differentiated from that of the Sherden) could not be ascertained, and will be possible only after a study of this culture at other contemporary sites in the Sea Peoples' conjectured areas of settlement.

In addition to Dor, which was the center city of the Sikils in the region, pottery and other artifacts of the Northern Sea Peoples are known from excavations in the environs of the Sharon.

At *Tel Ḥefer*, excavations revealed "disturbed context and a few pits which were dug into the destruction of the Late Bronze (Stratum A/6) where a few sherds of 'Philistine' pottery were also recovered" (Paley and Porath 1993:612–613).

At *Tel Zeror* in the Sharon Plain, several strata belonged to the Iron Age I, although the exact date of each stratum is not clear. The early Iron Age settlement is represented by refuse pits dug into the ruins of the Late Bronze Age II public building. The pits contained bones of sheep, goats, and cattle and sherds of bowls, pithoi, and cooking pots typical of the twelfth century BCE. In the cemetery, about ten graves of children and adults buried in collared-rim pithoi belong to this period. Burials from the eleventh and early tenth centuries BCE include nine large cist tombs built of stone and covered with large stone slabs. The wealth of funerary offerings in these family tombs included "Philistine" pottery, bell-shaped bowls, shafted spear heads, and a clay cup in the shape of a lioness of the type often found in strata of the Sea Peoples. Contemporary with these burials is the eleventh-century BCE citadel with a casemate wall of large bricks built on the northern peak (Ohata 1967; 1970; Kochavi 1993). It seems, however, that only a small number of vessels here could be definitely attributed to the Sea Peoples.

We should also point out that the material culture of the Sea Peoples is exibited along the eastern border of the Sharon Plain in, for example, the tombs excavated at Jatt (Artzy 2006) and Et-Tayiba (Yannai 2002).

Another site containing Sikil material is *Ein Hagit,* a rural settlement located in Wadi Milek on the ancient pass through the Carmel mountains that links the coastal site of Dor (just 12 km. to the west) with Yokne'am (8 km. to the northeast) and the Jezreel Valley. The site was excavated by S. Wolff in 1995. The excavations yielded impressive architectural and pottery remains of a small Iron Age I agricultural farmstead, as well as various "Philistine" decorated sherds alongside local late "Canaanite" ceramic types. The excavator suggested that the ceramic finds from Ein Hagit parallel the assemblage at Dor, which dates from the end of the twelfth and the eleventh century BCE. He also believes that the "Philistine" pottery from Ein Hagit (Fig. 12) may reflect Sikil penetration into the area and that politically it may have been part of the Sikil region of Dor (Wolff 1998; Cohen-Weinberger and Wolff 2001).

At *El-Aḥwat* which is situated above the Nahal 'Iron (Wadi 'Ara), its excavator A. Zertal, claimed that it was built by the Sherden, one of the Sea Peoples (Zertal 2008). Examining the finds I failed to find any such connection.

At *Shiqmona*, on the Carmel coast north of Tel Dor, the excavator, J. Elgavish, attributed three strata (15, 14, and 13) to the Iron Age I. Elgavish associated the lowest of these strata with the Sea Peoples, but since the material of this period has not yet been published, final judgment must await its publication (Elgavish 1994:47).

To this list of the Sharon and Carmel coastal settlements, we should perhaps add the ships' engravings on the rocks of the Carmel ridge not far from the famous Carmel Caves and almost opposite Tel Nami (Fig. 13).

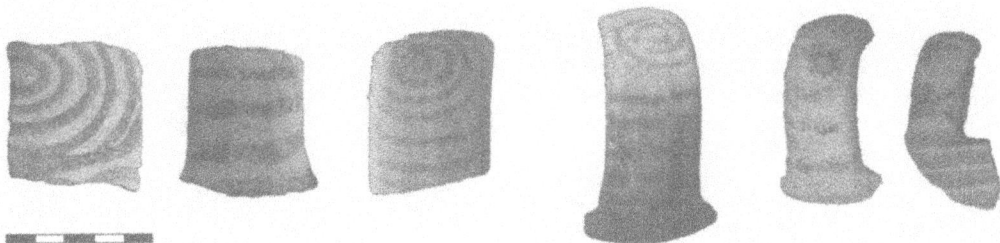

Figure 12 : "Sikil" pottery from Ein Hagit (the three on the left) and Dor (the three on the right).

M. Artzy believes that the engravings represent ships of the Sea Peoples, and that one in particular is reminiscent of the Sea Peoples' boats depicted on the Medinet Habu reliefs of Ramesses III (Artzy 1987; 2003; Wachsmann 1981; 1997).

Figure 13. A Carmel Ship.

It should be pointed out that excavations conducted at two sites on the coast on either side of Tel Dor—Tel Mevorakh to the south, excavated by the present writer, and Tel Nami, to the north, excavated by M. Artzy—revealed that both sites were destroyed at the end of the Late Bronze Age (i.e., at the end of the thirteenth or beginning of the twelfth century BCE), probably by the Sea Peoples, who did not rebuild them. Both sites showed a gap in settlement: Tel Nami was never reoccupied and Tel Mevorakh was resettled by the Phoenicians or Israelites only after a gap at the end of the eleventh or beginning of the tenth century BCE (Stern 1978; 1984; Artzy 1993; 1995).

THE PLAIN OF ʿAKKO

A preliminary report of a survey conducted by G. Lehmann in the ʿAkko valley sheds light on the settlement complexes of ʿAkko and surroundings. In the Late Bronze Age, the populated area of ʿAkko covered over 10 ha. and its settlement complex included 41 settlements. During the Iron Age I, the population in the ʿAkko valley decreased by ca. 10%-20%. The most significant change in the region, according to the survey, was the collapse of the settlement complex. ʿAkko ceased to be a large central city, while 38 settlements in the surveyed region were no more then villages. It also seemed to Lehmann that although the Sea Peoples settled in the northern coastal plain, the Canaanite culture remained dominant in the region (Lehmann 2001).

Excavations at three sites in the Plain of ʿAkko uncovered remains of the Sea Peoples: ʿAkko, Tell Keisan, and Tell Abu Hawam (see Fig. 2). The Sea Peoples at these sites are believed to be the Sherden mentioned in the Onomasticon of Amenope (see above).

Tel ʿAkko was excavated by M. Dothan. The findings from the relevant strata are complex, but several areas provide clear evidence of the presence of the Sea Peoples (M. Dothan 1976; 1986; 1993). According to Dothan, after the end of the Late Bronze Age city, a new population arrived at ʿAkko and made use of several of the existing installations. The final publication of the excavation has not yet appeared, but Dothan published a handful of what he called "Mycenaean IIIC:1b" sherds from the site. Some of the sherds had been found not far from a potter's kiln in Area B (see here Fig. 14 and M. Dothan 1986:106; 1989:60; Dothan and Dothan 1992: 213–215). These sherds are fragments of painted monochrome (red-brown or black) bell-shaped bowls, a krater, and some closed vessels, including a stirrup vase (M. Dothan 1989:61, Fig. 3.1; 62, Fig. 3.2). He noted that their shape and decoration (i.e., chevrons, net-filled lozenges, hatched triangles, antithetic tongues, scales, spirals, a bird, etc.) were of Aegean inspiration (ibid:60), Because of the proximity of some of the sherds to the potter's kiln, Dothan considered them locally made and associated them with the settlement of the Sherden Sea Peoples in the Plain of ʿAkko (see below, and also Yasur-Landau 2006).

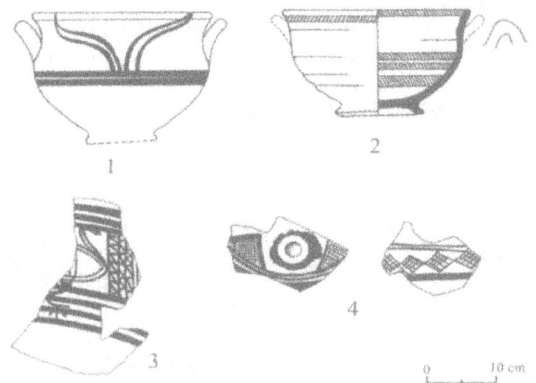

Figure 14. ʿAkko: Late "Mycenaean" pottery vessels.

Another important find believed to belong to the Sea People population of 'Akko was a stone vessel in a shape of a mortar that apparently served as a portable altar. One side features an incised depiction of several row-boats or sailboats (see here Fig. 15; Artzy 1987; 2003).

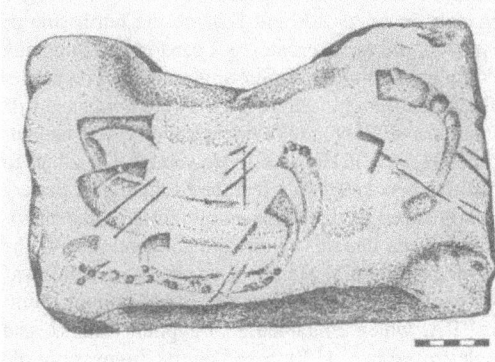

Figure 15. The 'Akko Boats.

As at Tel Dor, here too were found numeous fragments of bronze and copper vessels on a charred flagstone pavement, two burned and charred clay-smelting crucibles with remains of copper adhering to their inner walls, fragments of clay blast pipes (tuyeres) used for smelting, and copper slag and fragments of flawed metal vessels that were apparently destined for recycling.

The occupants of 'Akko in the early Iron Age (in Areas A, B, A-B and F) built their homes on top of the old ramparts, which had by then lost their defensive character; they were apparently engaged mainly in craft production. In M. Dothan's view, the archaeological finds—workshop installations, pottery kilns, and incised drawings of ships on the altar—all seem to attest to the arrival, perhaps by sea, of a new population group in the city after the end of the Late Bronze Age.

Tell Keisan. At this mound located in the northern part of the Plain of 'Akko, several kilometers east of 'Akko, a French expedition conducted extensive excavations over a period of many years (for the final excavation reports, see Briend and Humbert 1980; Humbert 1981; 1988; 1993; Balensi 1981).

The excavations at Tell Keisan were similar to those at Dor in that they too did not penetrate into the Late Bronze Age strata. According to the excavators, Strata 13–10 could be dated to the twelfth century BCE (despite the scant finds), Stratum 9 consisted of three phases

from the eleventh century and Stratum 8 was ascribed to the transition period between the eleventh and the tenth centuries BCE. "Philistine" pottery found at the site was considered by the excavators to be of local manufacture (Humbert 1988:72), and thus not strictly "Philistine" (Briend 1980:210 and 229). The question of whether or not the excavators envisaged a Sea Peoples' presence at the site remains somewhat open, although Humbert has suggested that Stratum 13 may have been destroyed by Sea Peoples (1988:72-73,76).

The pottery of these strata was reexamined by one of the expedition members and formed the subject of his Ph.D. dissertation (Burdajewicz 1992; 1994). His conclusions, for the most part, confirmed those of the excavators but he disagreed with them on one point: He dated Stratum 9 and its three phases to the first three quarters of the eleventh century and moved Stratum 8 forward to the last quarter of the eleventh century, and its end to the beginning of the tenth century. The stratum most relevant to our discussion and containing the richest material of the Sea Peoples is Stratum 9, with its three phases, whose destruction was ascribed by Burdajewicz to c. 1025 (in his opinion, corresponding to Tell Abu Hawam IV, Megiddo VIA and Tell Qasile X).

Thus, the finds associated with the Sea Peoples were scattered throughout the excavated areas at Tell Keisan in all three phases of Stratum 9 (with a small number also appearing in Stratum 8), but the most important and homogeneous material for our subject was uncovered in Pit 6067 of Stratum 9C (Briend and Humbert 1980, Pls. 67, 70, 74–75, 78).

Tell Abu Hawam. This large mound, located at the mouth of the Kishon, in the southern part of the 'Akko Plain, was excavated by several expeditions, the first directed by R. W. Hamilton, who attributed two strata to the Early Iron Age: Stratum IV to 1230–1100 and Stratum III to 1100–925 BCE. He dated Stratum V to the end of the Late Bronze Age (Hamilton 1935). Many years ago, B. Mazar suggested that, on the basis of a reexamination of the finds, a gap in settlement existed between c. 1175 and 1050 BCE (Maisler 1951).

In renewed excavations conducted by a French expedition, additional phases of occupation from the Early Iron Age were noted. The excavator, J. Balensi, distinguished between early Stratum VC which, in her opinion, still belonged to the final phase of the Late Bronze Age, and late Stratum VC, which she attributed to the early Iron Age, but to a relatively late phase since it lacked certain features of the early phases. Because of the absence of these features, she claimed that a gap existed between the two phases and that the late VC phase should be ascribed to the end of the twelfth century. She also divided Stratum IV into five separate phases, dating the first two phases to the eleventh century and the last three to the end of the eleventh and beginning of the tenth century (Balensi 1980; 1981; 1985; Balensi and Herrera 1985; 1993). All the excavators unanimously agreed that the early part of the twelfth century was missing at the site and the beginning of the Iron Age occupation occurred at the end of the twelfth or even the beginning of the eleventh century.

The finds associated with the Sea Peoples at Tell Abu Hawam come mainly from Strata V and IV. According to Balensi, sherds were recovered that "are possibly Philistine" (Balensi 1993:13) and it can be assumed that the reference is to vessels with monochrome decoration. Among the noteworthy finds which, in our opinion, should be attributed to the Sea Peoples' occupation of the city are two Cypriot cylinder seals of the type found at Tel Dor (one of which was in fact assigned to the Iron Age I in the excavation report), and local libation vessels in the form of a bull decorated with a red monochrome net pattern (almost identical to the bull figurine from Tel Dor and cf. Hamilton 1935:41, Fig. 248 and Pl. 38:217, here Fig. 45:2-3).

In recent excavations at Tell Abu Hawam, directed by M. Artzy, red monochrome sherds in the Northern Sea Peoples' style which were uncovered at the site could also be attributed to this phase (Artzy, personal communication).

THE WESTERN JEZREEL VALLEY

Large-scale excavations have been conducted at almost all the important mounds in the western Jezreel Valley: Megiddo, Yokne'am, Tel Qiri, Tel Qashish and Afula, and also at a few of the smaller mounds. "Philistine" pottery vessels, bichrome and mainly red monochrome, were found in all the Iron Age I strata at these sites.

Megiddo. This site was without doubt the main settlement of the Sea Peoples in the region (Lamon and Shipton 1939; Loud 1948); however, the history of the excavation of Stratum VI at Megiddo is one of the most complicated and difficult to unravel in the archaeology of Palestine. The remains uncovered in Stratum VI at Megiddo and their historical significance have been the subject of the most intensive and drawn-out debate in the annals of Israeli archaeology (cf. Mazar 2002:275-276; idem 2007; and see below).

Stratum VI was first uncovered by G. Schumacher (in whose stratigraphical system it was designated Stratum IV). In the extensive excavations carried out by the Oriental Institute of the University of Chicago in the 1920s and 1930s, this stratum was excavated in several areas and divided into two phases: VIB and VIA. However, only in Areas AA and DD, on the north side of the mound, did the excavators succeed in assigning any building remains to the earlier Stratum VIB. The wealth of finds discovered in Stratum VIA were published first by Lamon and Shipton (1939) and Loud (1948), and later, in 2004, in T. P. Harrison's *Megiddo 3.* The Chicago expedition concluded only that the Stratum VIA pottery was influenced by the Canaanite culture of the previous period and that this culture did not continue into the following Stratum V. Harrison, on the other hand, was more explicit in his conclusions: In his opinion, Stratum VIIA, which contained an Egyptian fortress, and was destroyed in c. 1130 (based on the discovery of the bronze statue of Ramesses VI; and cf. Ussishkin 1995) and Stratum VIA, which was sealed by a thick layer of destruction on which Stratum VB was built. Harrison, as well as L. Stager in a preface to the book, has no hesitation in retaining the conventional destruction date of Stratum VIA to the early tenth century BCE and attribute it to David's conquest (Harrison 2003; 2004).

In the 1960s, Y. Yadin renewed excavations at Megiddo (Yadin 1970), penetrating down to Stratum VI. He, too, was of the opinion that Stratum VIA represented the last Canaanite stratum in the city and was destroyed during the conquests of David. Yadin did not manage to publish his final report before his death and it was completed by A. Zarzecki-Peleg (1997a; 2005), who agreed with Yadin's chronological and historical conclusions (see below).

T. Dothan, in her comprehensive and detailed treatment of the remains of the Philistine material culture at this site, was of the opinion—following the excavators—that Iron Age I at Megiddo, represented by the three strata, VIIA, VIB and VIA, spanned a period from the twelfth to the late eleventh century BCE. From her study of the finds, she concluded that "Philistine" cultural influence was present from Stratum VIIA to the end of Stratum VIA. It should be noted that, in addition to the few bichrome "Philistine" vessels, numerous monochrome (red or black) decorated vessels of the Northern Sea Peoples' type were found at the site. Also uncovered here were cult vessels and artifacts unique to the Sea Peoples, such as a lioness-shaped rhyton, a dozen or more "wall brackets," some decorated with applied bull protomai, bronze double axes, and a handle of a typical iron knife (T. Dothan 1982:72–74; idem, 1989a; Brug 1985:48; Harrison 2004; Mazar 2007; and see below).

Another theory proposed by A. Kempinski on this subject should also be noted here. He suggested that Stratum VIA at Megiddo had been destroyed in an earthquake in the middle of the eleventh century BCE (Kempinski 1989), but this theory is not usually accepted.

A. Mazar later argued that the local material culture of the latest Iron Age I stratum—VIA—consisted of three components: The first, the bulk of the pottery, was of local Canaanite origin and continued the local Late Bronze Age traditions; it provided evidence of the presence of a Canaanite population in the city up to the time of its destruction (Mazar 1980:1985a; 1985b;

1994; 2002; 2007). The second component was Phoenician. The third cultural component of Megiddo VIA, according to Mazar, is that of Cypriot or Aegean origin. He mantioned a notable resemblance between Megiddo VI and Tell Qasile X in many details, including shapes of loom weights, pottery types, decorative style (such as the appearance of a krater decorated with isolated spirals in black color) and the so-called "Orpheus Jug" (here Fig. 16), a painted strainer jug depicting a procession of animals and a lyre-player in front of a sacred tree (Mazar 2007:85; cf also in this matter: Yasur-Landau in: Fatalkin and Yasur-Landau 2008:214-229; idem, 2009). Mazar adds to this list the appearance of baths and bronze objects (such as a double-axe, axe-adzes and shafted spear heads); and continues:

Figure 16. The "Orpheus" jug from Megiddo.

The significance of these resemblances [between Megiddo VIA and Qasile X] is not so clear. . . . The title "Philistine" used for some of these components . . . is questionable. Though one cannot speak confidently of the presence of Philistines at Megiddo, it is tempting to think that certain elements in the material culture of Megiddo VI are due to some presence of a Cypriot/Aegean population at Megiddo, alongside the Canaanite majority. (Mazar 2007: 85)

It appears that whereas Stratum VIIA was either an Egyptian stronghold (Ussishkin 1995) or a "Canaanite" town (Mazar 2002), Stratum VIB can be considered a Sea Peoples' town, and Stratum VIA may also have been occupied by Sea Peoples, but alongside a mixed (Canaanite-Phoenician) population, i.e., the same phenomena can be found here that were detected by A. Mazar at Tell Qasile X and other excavators at Tell Keisan 9 and Tell Abu Hawam late V and IV, and by myself at Tel Dor (Mazar 1980; 1985a; 1985b; 1994:41–42; 2002; 2007; see also Miron 1985 and Stern 2000a). In the latest excavations at Megiddo directed by I. Finkelstein and D. Ussishkin, similar finds were uncovered (Finkelstein et al. 2000; Arie 2004; 2006).

Remains dating to Iron Age I were also found in Areas K, M, F, and L. According to the excavators, fragmentary remains of a domestic building were unearthed in Area K, Level K-5 (Stratum VIB). This level also produced a unique, locally-made stirrup-jar in Mycenaean IIIC style (Yasur-Landau 2006; and see detailed discussion below), as well as evidence of metallurgical activity (similar to the finds from Dor and Tel 'Akko).

A large domestic building, featuring a central courtyard surrounded by nine rooms, was built in Level K-4 (Stratum VIA). The building was destroyed in a fierce conflagration, with the destruction debris reaching one meter in some places. It yielded a rich assemblage of pottery. In Area M, an elaborate building of Level M-4 (VIA) is being excavated. This building, too—like the entire city of this period—came to an end in a tremendous conflagration, its debris consisting of mud bricks almost petrified by the flames and over one meter thick.

In Area F, the remains of Level F-6 (VIB) consisted of a single tomb. Simple domestic houses were constructed here in Level F-5 (VIA); the town of this period was the last to occupy both the upper and lower mounds. Burnt remains of this city were also uncovered in Area L (Level L-5) beneath Palace 6000.

Controversy surrounding the chronology of Stratum VI at Megiddo arose when I. Finkelstein, even before his excavations at Megiddo, published a series of articles in which he sought to disprove the unanimously accepted

basis of the absolute chronology of the Iron Age. Finkelstein adopted a Low Chronology, lowering the traditional dates by seventy years (Finkelstein 1995; 1996; 2005; 2006; 2009). He has reiterated his theory on numerous occasions, restating it in the first volume of the excavation report published by the Tel Aviv Megiddo expedition (Finkelstein et al. 2000; Finkelstein 2006). In his opinion, Megiddo does not serve as a reliable chronological peg between Strata VIIA and III, that is, between the time of Ramesses III and the campaigns of the Assyrian kings at the end of the eighth century BCE. He rightly claimed that the only key for dating the strata at Megiddo is through the "Philistine" pottery, which he believed is restricted to Stratum VIB, while the "Philistine" pottery from Stratum VIA is composed mainly of degenerated forms, similar to, or even later than, Stratum X at Tell Qasile. He therefore ascribed Stratum VIB at Megiddo to the eleventh-tenth centuries BCE and Stratum VIA to the middle of the tenth century and its destruction to Shishak's campaign in 925 BCE. (But see his recent articles: Finkelstein 2006:181-182 and especially Finkelstein and Piasetzky 2008; 2009 where he himself rejects this date).

E. Arie studied the "Philistine" pottery of Megiddo and came to two conclusions: That the "Philistine" ceramic material found in situ was confined in the site only to Stratum VI (both phases; cf. also Mazar 2002), and Finkelstein's (2006) attempt to distinguish pure (VIB) from degenerate (VIA) "Philistine" pottery for chronological purposes should be rejected (Arie 2006:222-223; and cf. also Halpern 2009).

Finkelstein's chronological suggestions were challenged not only by Stager and Harrison, but also by A. Mazar, who recently claimed that a confirmation of the conventional chronology was available from the Tel Aviv excavations at Megiddo themselves, according to new C[14] dates (Mazar 1997, 2005; 2007:85-86; Mazar and Bronk Ramsey 2008; and see also Singer-Avitz 2009), and again by A. Ben-Tor and A. Zarzecki-Peleg, who also fixed the stratigraphy of three sites adjoining Megiddo: Tel Qiri, Yokne'am, and Tel Qashish (see below). Zarzecki-Peleg, who published the final report of the finds from Y. Yadin's excavations at Megiddo (Zarzecki-Peleg 2005; and see also 1997a; 1997b), concurred with Yadin's chronological conclusions at Megiddo (Yadin 1970) and Ben-Tor's correlations of Yokne'am, Qiri, and Hazor with Megiddo. Zarzecki-Peleg consequently dated Strata VIB and VIA at Megiddo to the eleventh century; she ascribed the destruction of Stratum VIA to the Israelite conquest, and correlated them with Strata XVIII and XVII at Yokne'am (and see also recently A. Mazar 2006:273; 2007:85-86).

In the opinion of the present writer, Finkelstein is correct in one of his claims, namely that the "Philistine" pottery, or more precisely the pottery of the Northern Sea Peoples at Megiddo (but as well as at Qiri, Yokne'am and Qashish and all the other sites in the Plain of 'Akko and the western Jezreel Valley) is the key to understanding the transition from the Iron Age I to the period of the monarchy. That is to say, any stratum containing "Philistine" finds could not have been under Israelite control, and vice versa: The earliest stratum at Megiddo without finds of this type should belong to the Israelites. At Megiddo there is no doubt that this transition occurred distinguished between Stratum VIA and Stratum V (and see most recently Leonard and Cline 1988, Harrison 2004; Arie 2004; Mazar 2007; Gilboa 2009).

In the mound of *Afula*, in the center of the Jezreel Valley, just a few kilometers north of Megiddo, M. Dothan exposed architectural remains of the Iron Age I (Stratum III). According to him, this stratum featured a main building of four broad rooms along three sides of a large courtyard; two floors, Strata IIIb and IIIa, could be distinguished in the building. Stratum IIIb, containing local pottery continuing the tradition of the previous Late Bronze Age, was dated to the first half of the twelfth century BCE. Stratum IIIa was dated by its "Philistine" ware to the eleventh century.

T. Dothan maintained that this "Philistine" pottery, which was only a small percentage of the whole, "lacks both in shape and decoration the elegance of the Philistine floruit and suggests an eleventh-century date" (T. Dothan 1982:80). It consisted mainly of decorated bowls and jugs. The pottery of Stratum IIIa spans most of the eleventh century BCE; the city was probably destroyed at the end of this century.

The excavation of the Iron Age I Eastern Cemetery at Afula yielded a relatively large assemblage of "Philistine" vessels which, on the whole, parallel those of Stratum IIIa, with the exception of one jug decorated with distinctive monochrome geometric designs (Fig. 17), about which T. Dothan wrote: "This jug, which is unique in shape and decoration, cannot be readily classified with any of the phases and styles of Philistine pottery although it belongs to a monochrome variant of Philistine pottery" (M. Dothan 1955:48–50, Fig 20; T. Dothan 1982:189). This is the same type of monochrome decoration found on the "Sikil" beer jug from Dor. Also of importance in this context was the discovery of a clay figurine in a style typical of the Sea Peoples (M. Dothan 1955:48–50, Fig. 20; T. Dothan 1982: 189; and cf. here Fig. 43:5).

Figure 17. Afula: The monochrome jug.

At *Yokne'am*, "Philistine" vessels (both monochrome and bichrome) were found in different areas of the Iron Age I in Strata XVIII–XVII (Fig. 18). The excavator, A. Ben-Tor, dated Stratum XVIII to the second half of the twelfth and beginning of the eleventh century BCE, and Stratum XVII to the second half of the eleventh century. He recognized that "one of the pottery groups resembles 'Philistine vessels'" (Ben-Tor 1993: 808).

Also discovered here was the head of a figurine in a marked Cypriot style, though it was attributed to the end of the Late Bronze Age (Ben-Tor et al. 2005: 9–89; Zarzecki-Peleg 1997b). According to A. Yasur-Landau all the "Philistine" vessels here are "extremely late eleventh century examples, with heavy Cypriot influence" (oral communication).

At nearby *Tel Qiri*, similar "Philistine" vessels were found in Strata IX-VIII, both dating to the Iron Age I (Ben-Tor and Portugali 1987: 101–103, 119, 126–128, and recently, Ben-Tor et al. 2005:169, fig. 42:1-7, here Fig. 19).

Figure 18. "Philistine" Vessels from Yokne'am.

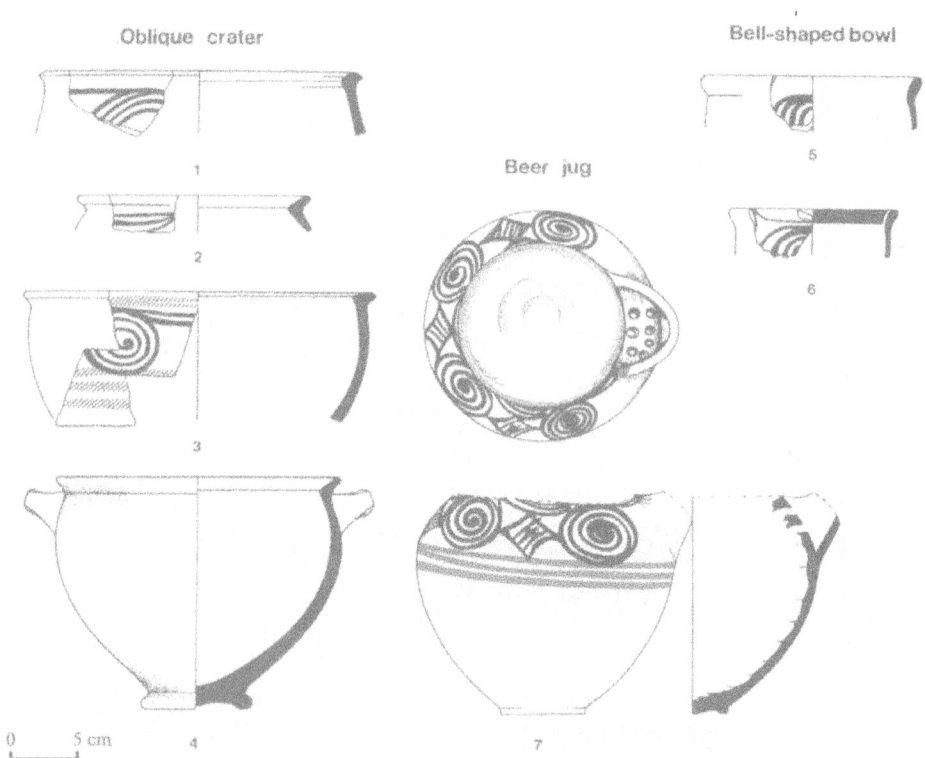

Figure 19. "Philistine" pottery from Tel Qiri.

At *Tel Qashish*, also in the vicinity of Yokne'am, remains of the early Iron Age settlement were exposed in three or four squares. Among the finds on the floors of a residential area (Stratum IV) were a few "Philistine" monochrome sherds (Ben-Tor et al. 2003: 344, Fig. 131:9, here Fig. 20).

In an extensive survey of the western Jezreel Valley, A. Raban found numerous "Philistine" sherds at various small sites (Raban 1991). At *Hurvat Hazin* (near the city of Tiveon), he uncovered remains of a fortification that contained "Philistine" ware, and in a trial excavation conducted in a small mound near Be'er-Tiveon, he discovered the lower part of a pit filled with broken pottery vessels, most of which he claimed were of the "Philistine" material culture, including a pyxis, a decorated bowl, and a large fragment of a "beer–jug" (Raban 1982: 24-29, XIII–XIV; 1991, Fig. 2). He unearthed similar ware at Tel Risim, Tel Re'ala (near Kfar Yehoshua), and at Hurvat Zeror, Tel Shan, Midrach Oz, and Tell Abu-Zureiq (near Tel Qiri). All these sites yielded various types of monochrome and bichrome pottery of the Sea Peoples (Fig. 21).

Recently a few more "Philistine" painted pottery sherds have been found at 'Ein el-Hilu (near Migdal HaEmeq) in the excavations of K. Covello-Paran (Fig. 22).

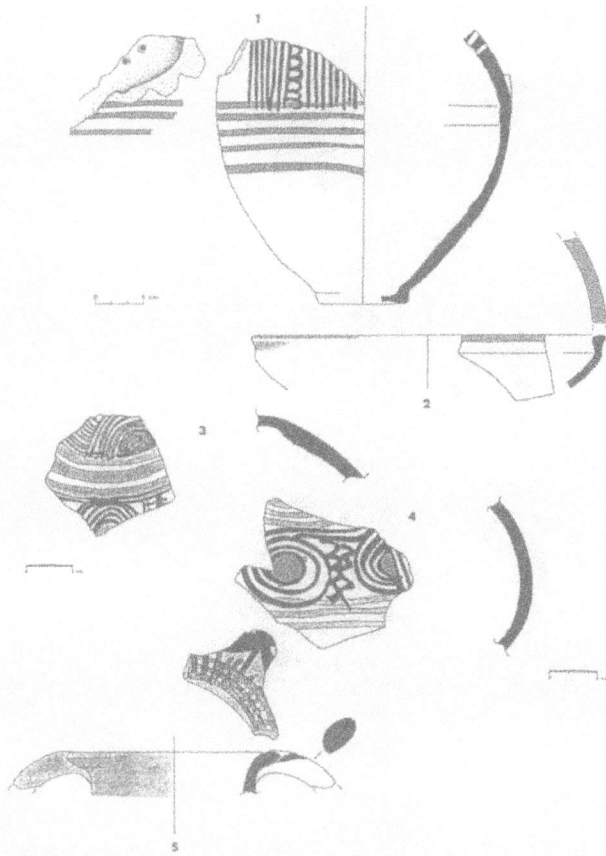

Figure 20. "Philistine" vessel from Tel Qashish.

Figure 21. "Philistine" pottery : 1-2 from Be'er Tiveon; 3 from Hurvat Hazin; 4-5 from Midrach Oz (according to A. Raban 1991).

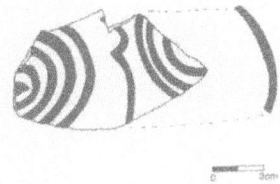

Figure 22. "Philistine" pottery sherds from 'Ein el-Hilu (Migdal HaEmeq).

3

THE POTTERY

INTRODUCTION

Much has been written about the unique nature of the material culture of the Philistines—the southern Sea Peoples—and especially about their pottery. Leading the field are the comprehensive studies of T. Dothan and her classic work on the subject, in which she summarized the manifold elements of its pottery and distinctive cult vessels, and, in a later series of articles, other characteristic aspects of this culture (T. Dothan 1982; 1989; 2000; 2002). A. Mazar followed with contributions to the subject after he had unearthed a rich assemblage of finds in excavations at Tell Qasile and carried out an exhaustive comparative study (A. Mazar 1980; 1985a; 1985b; and see also Pritchard 1968; Sandars 1985; Stager 1995; Ward 1998; Oren 2000; and many others too numerous to mention here).

Dothan's study also treated quite a few "Philistine" elements of the Northern Sea Peoples, mainly remains of the classic bichrome group of Philistine pottery which had made its way northward, and she occasionally also discussed other types of vessels which we here attribute exclusively to the Northern Sea Peoples.

It fortunately fell to my lot to direct the large-scale excavations at Tel Dor for twenty years (1980–2000), the city which, according to the sole detailed Egyptian source, the Wenamun Tale, was under the direct rule of the Sikils and their king Beder. Our discussion will therefore begin with Tel Dor.

In the excavations at Tel Dor, as we mentioned above, we penetrated in at least three different areas into remains of the Sikil settlement which contained large quantities of pottery and cult vessels typical of the Sikil culture. Other remains of this culture were uncovered in the mound in no clear stratigraphic context and also on surface level. The finds here, too, for the most part, consisted of two different types of assemblages: Pottery and cult vessels. The latter will be discussed below, as well as some other elements of this material culture.

Today, I admit my error: Throughout the many years of the excavations at Dor I thought—relying on T. Dothan's studies—that the meager bichrome ware found at the site was the only pottery that could be associated with the Sikils (Stern 2000a:94, Pl. I:2), though I realized that some of the sherds, especially the handles and body fragments decorated with characteristic "Philistine" designs (Stern 2000a:96; Fig. 47; Pl. IX:3–6), should also be attributed to the Northern Sea Peoples. These decorations include the antithetic, concentric, and other circles painted instead of the usual bichrome in red, or from a dark shade to an almost black hue (here fig. 12).

I began to reconsider my understanding of the finds from Dor for two reasons. At the end of the last sea-

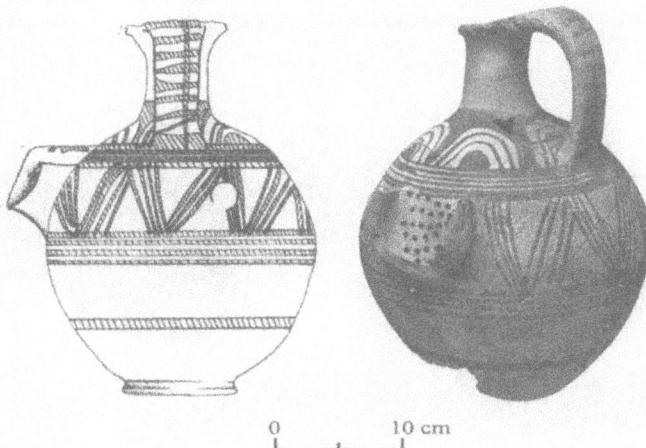

Figure 23. Dor: Monochrome "Sikil" strainer spout jug from Area G.

son of excavations, we submitted all the sherds of the "Philistine" bichrome ware for petrographic analysis (conducted by A. Cohen-Weinberger and Y. Goren), which revealed that the majority of these sherds were manufactured on the southern coast, within the traditional Philistine area of settlement, and were brought to the northern coast, that is, they were not produced by the Northern Sea Peoples (and see now Gilboa, Cohen-Weinberger, and Goren, 2006:314).

A complete strainer-spout jug was found in the Sikil stratum in Area G, decorated with semi-circles, etc. (Stern 2000a:Pl. IX:6; and here Fig. 23), which were fully consistent with the Philistine bichrome pottery repertoire but were executed here in red only. I sent a photo of the jug to V. Karageorghis, and he suggested that I compare it with jugs discovered at Enkomi, Cyprus, in Stratum 1a (from the Late Cypriote IIIB), which dates to the beginning of the eleventh century BCE. And, indeed, the similarity is striking. The petrographic analysis, however, indicated that the vessel was locally produced on the northern coast of Palestine; the vessel was apparently a local imitation of a Cypriot prototype. Fragments of two other vessels were later uncovered in the same Area G, which, at first glance, because of the outstanding quality of the paint, I was convinced were Cypriot imports. One of the sherds was a small fragment of a stirrup vase and the others were parts of a krater. Both of these vessels also bore painted decorations in red only (Stern 2000a, Pl. IX:1, here Fig. 24).

Here, too, the petrographic analysis revealed that the vessels were local imitations of an early, rare type of Cypriot pottery (of the twelve–eleventh centuries BCE), as I was informed in a letter by Maria Iacovou, an expert in

this period of Cypriot pottery, to whom I had sent their photos (cf. also Iacovou 1992; 1994; 1999).

After these two discoveries, the road to final enlightenment was short. It was now clear to me that, with the exception of a meager amount of bichrome ware imported from Philistia, the Northern Sea Peoples used similar vessels decorated with identical motifs, of which the majority were of western origin (from Mycenae or Cyprus), whose distinguishing feature was a red-painted monochrome decoration! Furthermore, in contrast to the relatively early monochrome decoration of Mycenaean IIIC ware and their imitations known from Philistia (Killebrew 2000:233–253; Dothan and Zukerman 2004; Sherratt, forthcoming), this decoration was of later date in the north; it was contemporaneous with, and closely paralleled, the Philistine bichrome decorated vessels widespread at the end of the twelfth and the eleventh centuries BCE. At present, no finds at Dor can be attributed with certainty to the monochrome phase of Philistine pottery (or to that corresponding to Mycenaean IIIC). The necessary conclusion is that the major settlement of the Sea Peoples in the north of Palestine commenced only at the end of the twelfth century and was mainly founded in the beginning of the eleventh.

Indeed, the INAA analyses of the "red" pottery showed that it was manufactured, almost in its entirety (despite its "Philistine" appearance), on the northern coast of Palestine. Only a few isolated vessels originated in Cyprus itself (Gunneweg and Perlman 1994).

After arriving at this new understanding of the origin of this pottery, I began to search for comparative material at additional northern sites which contained strata from this period and whose finds

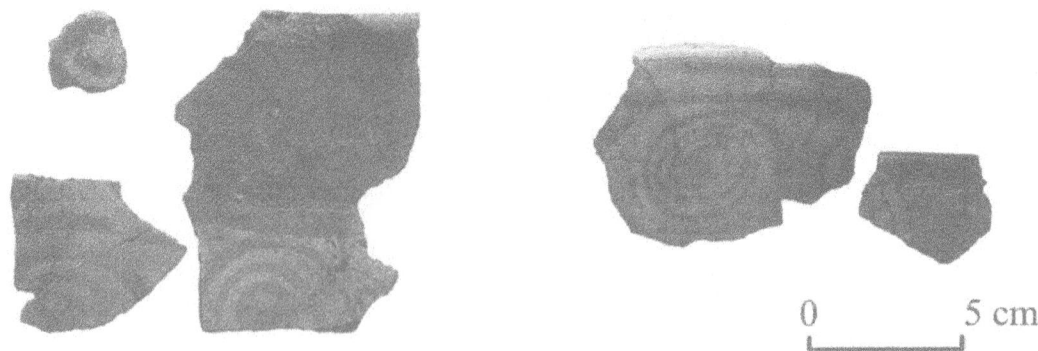

Figure 24. Dor: Local "Sikil" imitation of Cypriot pottery. On the left a stirrup vase and a krater, and monochrome "Sikil" sherds on the right.

had been fully or partly published. These sites, as was noted above, included 'Akko, Tell Keisan, Tell Abu Hawam, Tel Zeror and Tel Ḥefer (all located along the coast), Megiddo, Tel Qashish, Tel Qiri, Yokne'am and Afula in the western Jezreel Valley, and Ein Hagit in Wadi Milek, and perhaps also at Jatt and Tayiba, east of this line. It immediately became apparent that there was a very large group of vessels which fell into a separate group and which had to be reclassified in order to grasp its significance.

The most beautiful and comprehensive group of this type of pottery came not from Tel Dor, but from Tell Keisan, in the northern part of the 'Akko Plain. An especially large number of these vessels were uncovered in the three phases of Stratum 9. Of particular interest were the vessels recovered from Pit 6067 (Stratum 9C; Briend and Humbert 1980, Pls. 67,70,74–75,78), which consisted exclusively of a large number of "red" vessels. This assemblage represents the key to the understanding of the northern group of this pottery. Of equal importance were the finds from the excavations at Afula, on the mound itself and in the eastern cemetery, which also yielded numerous vessels of this type. Other important material, of course, came from parallel strata at Megiddo, especially the two phases of Stratum VI, of which a large assortment of decorated types in this distinctive style have been published (and see the above discussion of these sites).

T. Dothan, in her discussion of the finds from Afula, also realized the unique quality of this northern pottery, especially of a jug that resembles the jug from Dor (and cf. here Figs. 17 and 23) stated:

> The excavation of the Iron Age I eastern cemetery has provided a collection of Philistine vessels that, on the whole, parallel those from stratum IIIa. The majority belongs to the debased phase of Philistine pottery, especially the bowl [here Fig. 27:1–2]. A jug [here Fig. 17], unique in shape and decoration, cannot be readily classified with any of the phases and styles of Philistine pottery, although it belongs to the monochrome variant of Philistine pottery, which may reflect an early phase. (T. Dothan 1982:81)

A. Raban, who conducted a survey of all the sites from this period in the western Jezreel Valley reached a similar conclusion and noted (referring particularly to the jug from Afula):

> Though the summary of pottery samples described above includes mostly the typical Philistine bichrome ware, other types of decorated pottery of the earliest phase of the Iron Age were found at some sites in the same context. Those variants are monochrome decorated vessels of shapes similar to those decorated in Philistine style and with the same motifs. This stylistic variant is generally accepted among scholars as "locally made Mycenean III C-lb" pottery and is considered a benchmark for the presence of Sea Peoples in Palestine (and see also T. Dothan 1982:295; 1989; M. Dothan 1986; Kempinski 1985). (Raban 1991:23)

While in Philistia proper the monochrome style probably predates the true Philistine bichrome (T. Dothan 1989b), at the sites in the Jezreel Valley it was found in the same strata. Such is the case for Stratum VIa at Megiddo (Loud 1948, Pls. 69:7, 138:20, 140:23–25, 247:7, etc.), the jug from Afula (M. Dothan 1955, Fig. 23:1), and several vessels from Level VI at Beth Shan (Hankey 1982). Recent excavations along the northern coast of Israel ('Akko, Tell Keisan, Dor, Tell Abu-Hawam) prove that this common context of bichrome Philistine ware and monochrome Mycenean Ill-lb (either locally made or Cypriot) are characteristic of the twelfth century BCE (Balensi 1981; Balensi and Herrea 1985: 106–109; 1993). Such occurrences have been considered an indication of the presence of Sea Peoples other than Philistines in northern Israel.

A. Mazar too, in his review of *Megiddo* 3 remarks: "A certain amount of Philistine and related pottery (in Megiddo) indicates relations with Philistia, as well as a certain amount of local production of painted pottery decorated with motifs that resemble, but are not identical, to Philistine pottery" (Mazar 2007:84).

Recently, also A. Yasur-Landau, who studied the origins of the stirrup vase decorated with monochrome motifs uncovered in the latest excavations at Megiddo in Stratum K–5 (which corresponds to Stratum VIB, and see here Fig. 25) and the "Mycenaean" finds from 'Akko, noted that "a thin section analysis carried out by Y. Goren has shown that the vessel was made in the 'Akko plain, probably at 'Akko, Tell Keisan or their immediate vicinity" (Yasur-Landau 2006:300-301).

He adds:

> What was the inspiration for the creation of the Megiddo stirrup vase? Although there are no exact parallels, the combination of the paneled decoration filled with elaborate lozenges on the body of the vase and the joint, filled semicircles on its shoulder make it possible to identify the vessel as stemming from LH IIIC heritage. It is difficult, however, to assign it to a specific tradition. The lack of direct Cypriot parallels to the decoration brushes aside the possibility of an imitation of Mycenaean IIIC:Ib Cypriot imports. This probably also the case for LH IIIC pottery made in Tarsus in Cilicia. Considering the fact that Cypriot stirrup jars were indeed imported in the twelfth century

BCE to the 'Akko plain, The best-known example is the Tell Keisan stirrup jar (Balensi 1981; Gunneweg and Perlman 1994), which probably originated in Kouklia, Cyprus. The matte appearance of both slip and paint, as well as the red fabric of the vessel, may show some similarity to LH IIIC style pottery from Philistia (Mycenaean IIIC:1); however, to date there are no published parallels to the decoration of the Megiddo stirrup jar from Ashdod, Ashkelon, or Tel Miqne/Ekron. The similarity in motifs, and perhaps execution, to the Philistine Bichrome tradition is interesting. It is difficult to assume that the vessel is an imitation of Philistine Bichrome vessels produced in Philistia, because it does not resemble the northern production of bichrome vessels, as seen in Dor (Stern 1994:96, fig 47, attributed to the Sikila Sea People) and Dan (Biran 1994:126, fig. 87:3; Ilan 1999:93-95, pls.25:3; 59:1,7,8; 62:1; 65:6), whether imported from Philistia or locally made. Moshe Dothan published several "Mycenaean IIIC:1b" sherds from 'Akko. Some of them were found in connection with a potter's kiln in Area B (M. Dothan 1986:106; 1989: 60). They consist of fragments of monochrome-painted (black or red-brown ware), bell-shaped bowls, a krater, and some closed vessels, including a stirrup vase (M. Dothan 1989: 61, Fig. 3.1, 62; Fig. 3.2; [see here Fig. 10]). Dothan noted that their shape and decoration (e.g., chevrons, net-filled lozenges, hatched triangles, antithetic tongues, scales, spirals, a bird) were of Aegean inspiration (ibid: 60). The proximity of some of the sherds to the potter's kiln led him to consider them as locally made. Although a more detailed publication of the 'Akko Aegean-style pottery is needed, including a provenance study, it is evident that the style of some of the 'Akko pieces does not resemble the motifs found on LH IIC-style (Mycenaean IIC:1) pottery from Ashdod. The most obvious example is the bird fig-

ure on the krater fragment found in Area F (M. Dothan 1989: 62, Fig. 3.2d), which bears little resemblance to the Philistine birds. Therefore, there exists the option that the Megiddo stirrup jar belongs to a local production center of LH IIIC-style pottery in the 'Akko Plain that is neither directly influenced by Cypriot LH IIIC ("Mycenaean IIIC:1b") vessels nor by the Philistia LH IIIC ("Mycenaean IIIC:1") ware. (Yasur-Landau 2006:300-301)

At the end of his discussion Yasur-Landau comments that since the completion of his presentation in 2003, the decoration on the Megiddo stirrup jar is still without parallel in Philistia, even taking into account the many new examples published by Dothan and Zukerman in 2004 (Yasur-Landau 2006). But at the same time he claims that all these vases are but imitations of imports and not the produce of local Sea Peoples (oral communication).

A final remark concerning the uniquness of the pottery of the Northern Sea Peoples is taken from E. Arie's discussion. Arie, who dealt with the appearance of "Philistine Pottery" in Megiddo Stratum VI, concluded that:

> Eleven samples were taken from Philistine vessels or from vessels with Philistine-style decoration. Their types and decoration divide them into three classes: Closed vessels with Philistine Bichrome decoration on a white slip: only two strainer spouted jugs that were sampled belong to this class. The results indicate that both vessels were produced in the southern coast plain. Bell-shaped bowls decorated or non decorated: out of four

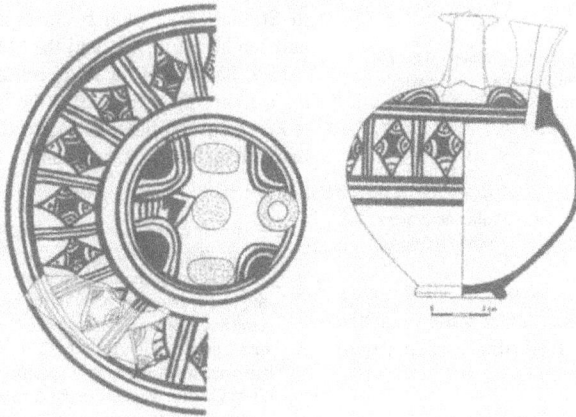

Figure 25. Megiddo: The monochrome stirrup vase from Stratum K–5.

two were produced in Philistia and the other two in the vicinity of Megiddo. Five vessels of various types with decoration reflecting Philistine influence: these vessels were produced in the immediate vicinity of Megiddo.

He adds:

Archaeometric studies of the Philistine vessels found outside the boundaries of Philistia reveal a similar picture: it was possible to divide the Philistine vessels into two groups: one brought from southern coastal plain and the other produced at the site itself or brought from other sites in the region. On the other hand, examination of the vessels found in Philistia revealed that Philistine vessels were made locally at the sites or were brought from other sites in Philistia. In addition, these studies have indicated a technological differentiation between Philistine wares and the Canaanite types in terms of raw material and firing temperatures. (Arie 2006:563-564)

A. Mazar (2002:274), identified this decorative style as part of the painted pottery tradition that characterizes the ceramic assemblage of the Iron Age I in the northern valleys. In the light of the Megiddo results it seems that they should be separated from the discussion of Philistine pottery production.

Thus, I am not the first to postulate the existence of a family of vessels unique to the Northern Sea Peoples. This pottery closely resembles but, at the same time, differs from the Philistine family of vessels, in that all its decorations are painted monochrome and occur in shades varying from red to black. It is contemporaneous with the Philistine bichrome ware, and also it is all locally made in the northern coast and valleys.

In our discussion of the unique characteristics of this pottery group, we should note that, like the Philistine bichrome ware, the pottery of the Northern Sea Peoples was influenced by three distinct pottery groups (it lacks the fourth group of vessels inspired by Egyptian pottery). The first group consists of vessels whose shapes are derived from the Mycenaean repertoire, the second are imitations of Cypriot prototypes, and the third group are ordinary local vessels but exhibit special features (such as horizontal handles) and especially decoration in the distinctive style of the Sea Peoples.

In the following, we will present a brief survey of the main types of the pottery of the southern Philistines; and the pottery of the Northern Sea Peoples, and the similarity or differences between the two groups.

PHILISTINE POTTERY FORMS

I do not intend to recapitulate T. Dothan's detailed treatment of each type of Philistine pottery but for purposes of our discussion will note here only that this pottery can be divided into two main groups: Vessels of Aegean origin, that is, Mycenaean or Cypriot, and local vessels with Philistine decorative motifs. (Vessels with Egyptian influence will not be discussed here.).

The main types of Mycenaean vessels preserved in the Philistine repertoire include:

1. Numerous variants of small bowls and kraters with horizontal handles (Fig.26:1–4).

2. Stirrup jars (Fig. 26:5–6).

3. Pyxides (Fig. 26:7–8).

4. Flasks (all the early Mycenaean types with the addition of a local variant with a spoon at the end; not included in Dothan's Philistines shapes) (Fig. 26:9–10).

5. Strainer-spout jugs of various types (Fig. 26:11).

6. Strainer-spout with basket handles (Fig. 26:12–13).

7. Three-handled jugs (Fig. 26:14).

Although neither the Late Bronze Age Cypriot lentoid flask nor bilbil jug was retained in the Philistine pottery repertoire, a variety of contemporaneous new vessels arrived from Cyprus of which the main types included:

8. Bottles of various types (Fig. 26:15–18).

9. Juglets with pinched bodies (Fig. 26:19–20).

All the other Philistine bichrome vessels are Egyptian (not discussed here) or local ware whose attribution to the Philistines is based on its decorative style, that is, to typical pseudo-Mycenaean motifs such as depictions of fish, and especially birds with heads turned back, and typical geometric motifs of antithetical concentric circles, cross-hatched or solid net, triangle or rhombus patterns, semicircles, Maltese crosses, hourglasses, etc. All these motifs are without doubt derived from the Cypriot or Late Mycenaean worlds.

Local vessels decorated with western designs are of the following types:

10. Bowls and kraters with upright handles.

11. A very rich assemblage of local jugs and juglets with handles extending to the rim or neck decorated in typical Philistine bichrome style or in a more complex bird and fish design (Fig. 26:21–23).

12. Jugs decorated in "Egyptian" style (Fig. 26:24).

13. Local storage jars decorated in "Philistine" style (Fig. 26:25).

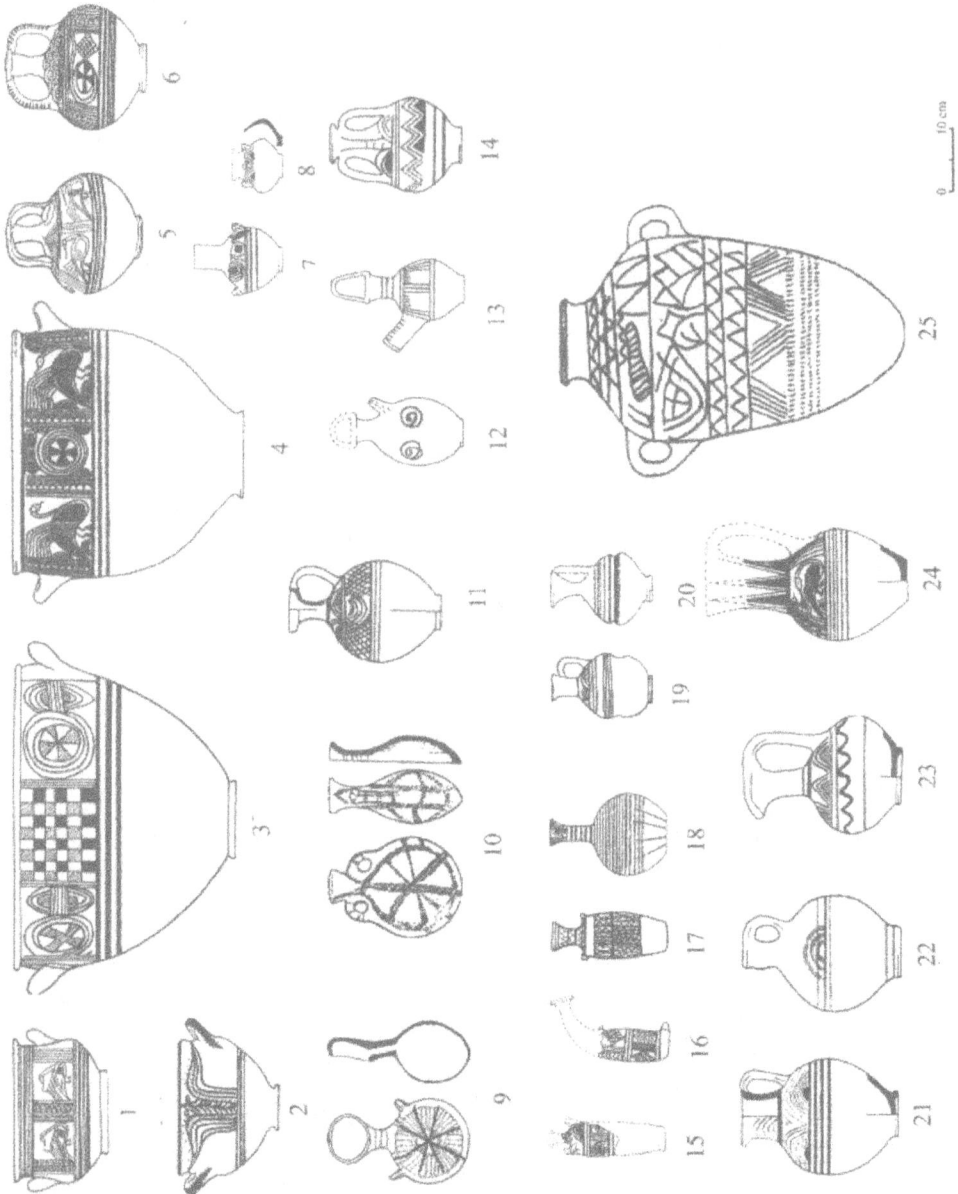

Figure 26. Philistine pottery vessel types.
1: Bowl from Gezer. 2: Bowl from Ashkelon. 3: Krater from Gezer. 4: Krater from Azor. 5: Stirrup jar from Gezer. 6: Stirrup jar from Beth-Shemesh. 7: Pyxis from Tell Beit Mirsim. 8: Pyxis from Gezer. 9: Flask from Gezer. 10: Flask from Qasile. 11: Strainer-spout jug from Tell el-Far'ah (S). 12: Jug from Gezer. 13: Jug from Tell el-Far'ah (S). 14: Three-handled jar from Tell Jemmeh. 15: Bottle from Tell eş-Şâfi/Gath. 16: Bottle from Beth-Shemesh. 17: Bottle from Gezer. 18: Bottle from Azor. 19: Juglet from Tell el-Far'ah (S). 20: Juglet from Gezer. 21: Jug from Beth-Shemesh. 22: Jug from Tell el-Far'ah (S). 23: Jug from Azor. 24: Jug from Tell el-Far'ah (S). 25: Jar from Tell el-Far'ah (S).

THE POTTERY OF THE NORTHERN SEA PEOPLES

When we come to examine the pottery types attributed here to the Northern Sea Peoples, an almost complete overlapping is revealed between the vessel types in the southern and the northern assemblages (with the exception, of course, of the monochrome painted decoration typifying the latter).

The northern repertoire can also be divided into two main groups: Vessels of Aegean origin, that is, either Mycenaean or Cypriot, and Local imitations decorated in the typical style of the Sea Peoples, but in *monochrome*.

The first group consists of the following vessels:

1. Bowls/kraters with horizontal handles

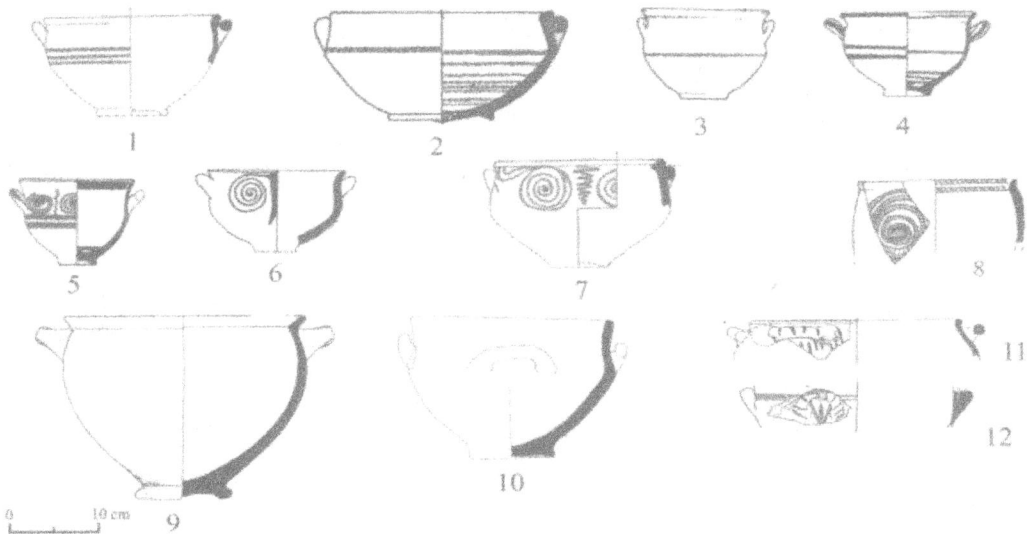

Figure 27. Monochrome decorated bowls and kraters with horizontal handles. 1–2, 7: 'Afula; 3: Beth-Shean; 4–6, 9–10: Megiddo; 8: Dor; 11–12: Tell Abu Hawam.

2. Stirrup jars

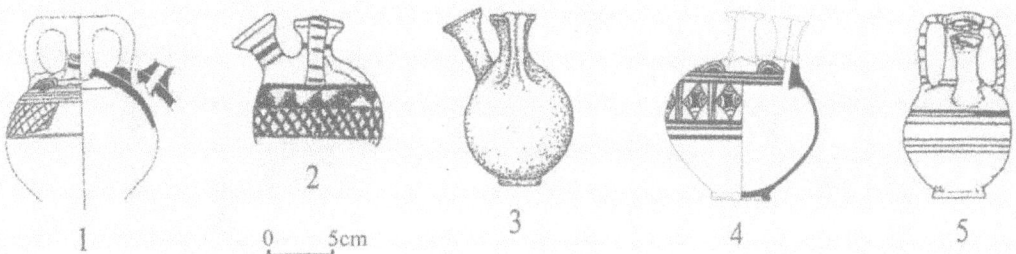

Figure 28. Monochrome decorated stirrup jars. 1: Tell Keisan; 2–4: Megiddo; 5: Yokne'am.

3. Pyxides

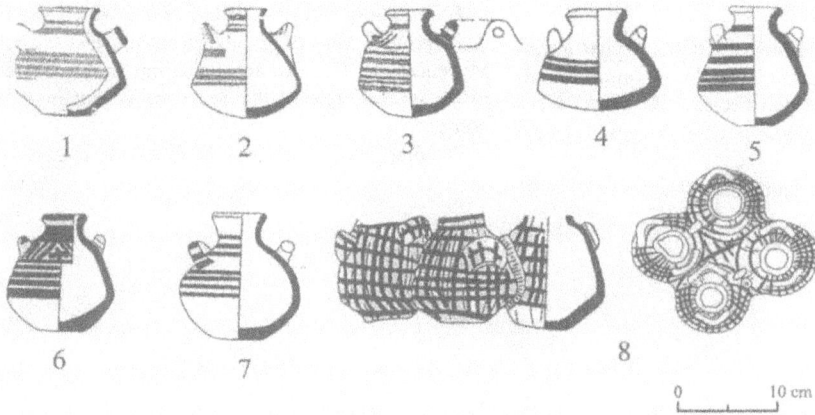

Figure 29. Monochrome decorated pyxides. 1: Tell Keisan; 2–3: Afula; 4–8: Megiddo.

4. Regular strainer-spout jugs

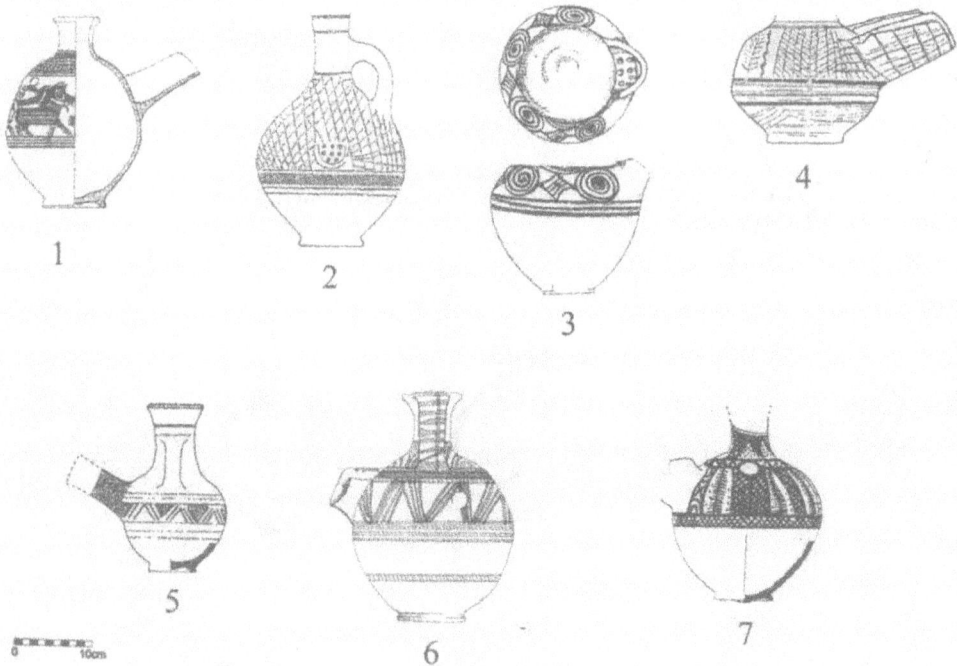

Figure 30. Monochrome decorated strainer-spout jugs. 1–2, 4–5, 7: Megiddo; 3: Tel Qiri; 6: Dor.

5. Strainer-spout jugs with basket handles

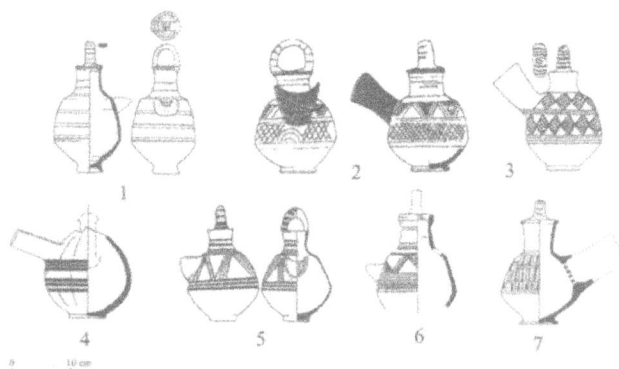

Figure 31. Monochrome decorated strainer-spout jugs with basket handles. 1–5: Megiddo; 6–7: Yokne'am.

6. Flasks, all types

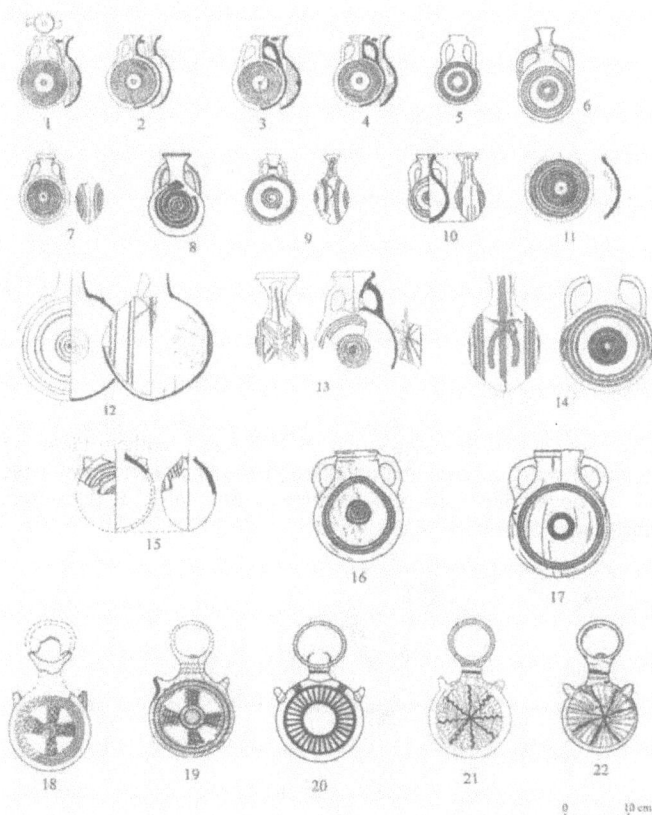

Figure 32. Monochrome decorated flasks. 1–4, 12–13: Tel Keisan; 5–6: Tell Abu Hawam; 7, 11, 14: Dor; 15: Afula; 16–17; 19–21: Megiddo; 18: Qiri; 22: Megiddo K–9.

To these should now be added new vessels of Cypriot
origin which were also common in the southern Philistine repertoire:

Bottles of various types

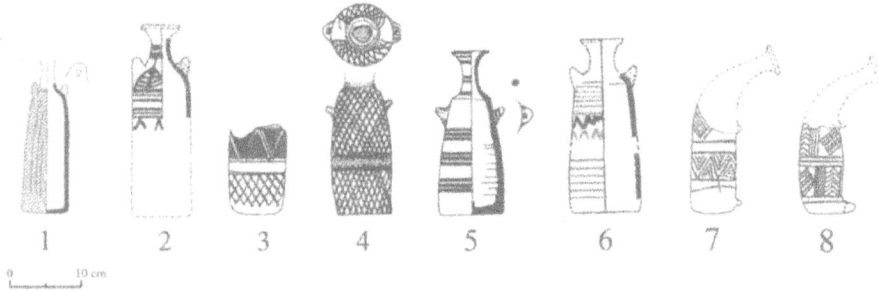

Figure 33. Bottles: 1–3, 6–8: Megiddo; 4–5: Yokne'am.

Juglet with pinched body

Figure 34. Decorated juglet with pinched body from Tell
Keisan.

The northern pottery, oddly enough, also included
a local variant of the Cypriot *bilbil* which has not yet
been encountered in the Philistine pottery repertoire of
the south and which we assumed above did not continue
into the Iron Age I southern Philistine pottery. Several
bilbils of this type decorated with typical red lines were
uncovered in Stratum 9C at Tell Keisan (Fig. 35).

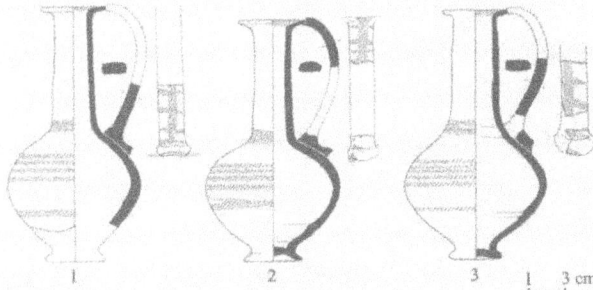

Figure 35. Monochrome decorated bilbils from Tell Keisan.

However, the largest group of decorated pottery in the unique style of the Northern Sea Peoples—similar to the Philistine ware—consists of ordinary local vessels which are differentiated from the other vessels only by the red decoration in the above-mentioned motifs.

We will mention here:

1. Numerous bowls with ordinary upright handles (Fig. 36:1, 3, 10–13), set on three feet (Fig. 36: 14-16), bar-handled (Fig. 36:6) and carinated bowls (Fig. 36: 4,9).

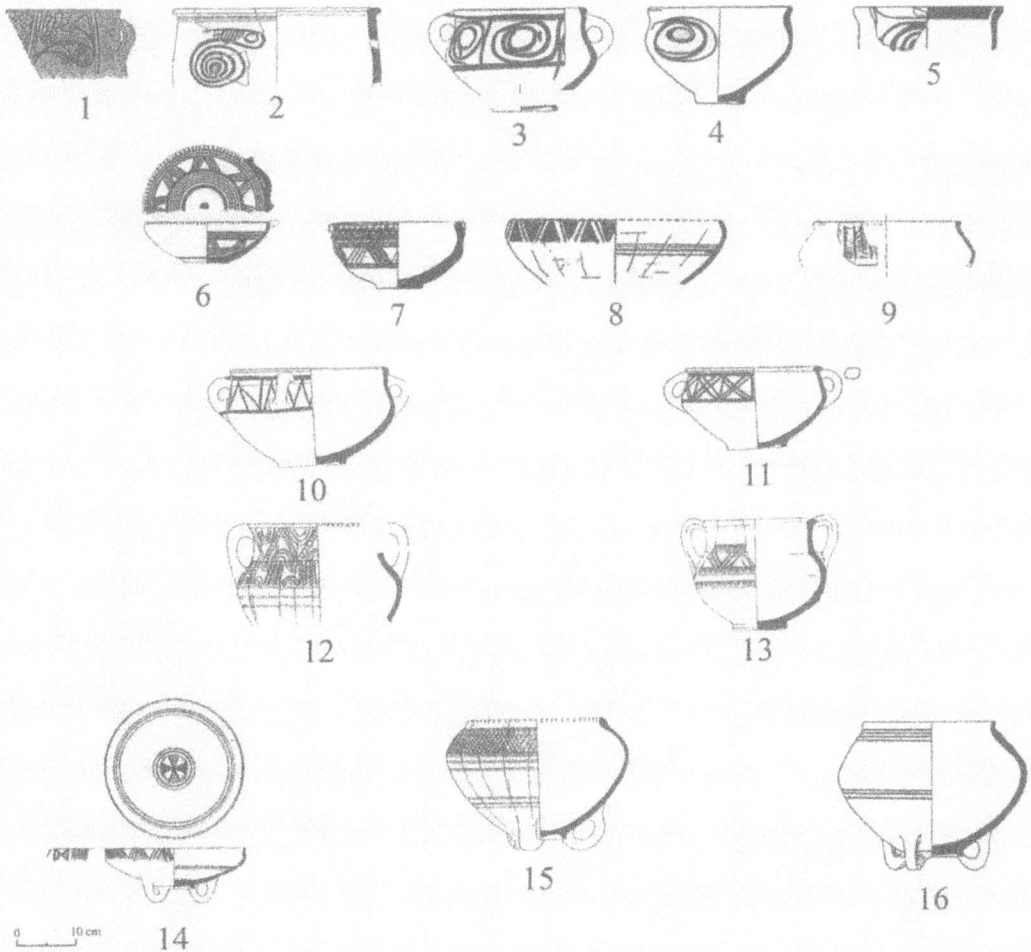

Figure 36. Monochrome decorated local bowls and kraters: 1: Tel Dan; 2: Keisan; 3–4, 6–8, 10-12, 14–16: Megiddo; 5, 13: Dor; 9: Tell Abu Hawam.

2. A diverse group of jugs and juglets.

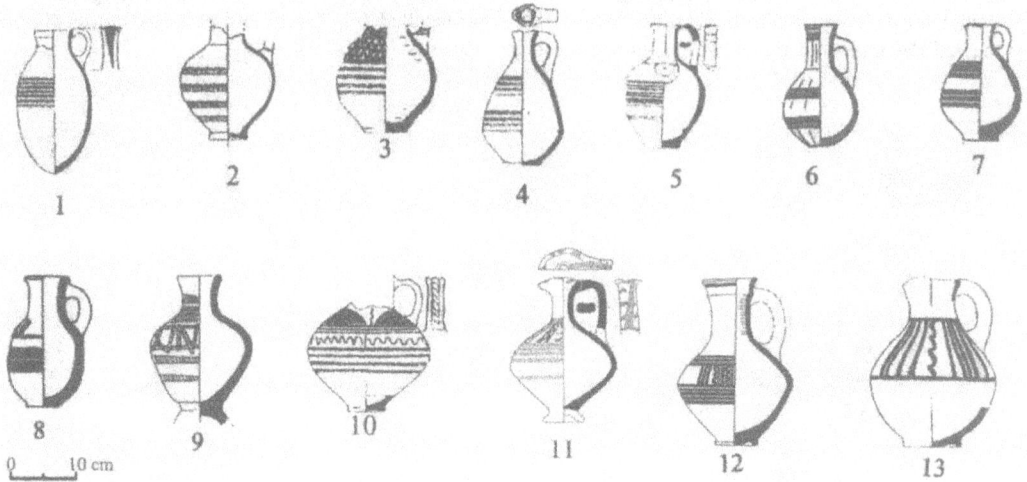

Figure 37. Monochrome decorated local jugs and juglets: 1, 10: Afula; 2: Tell Abu Hawam; 3, 9: Dor; 4-5: Tel Qiri; 6–8, 12–13: Megiddo; 11: Keisan.

3. Jars.

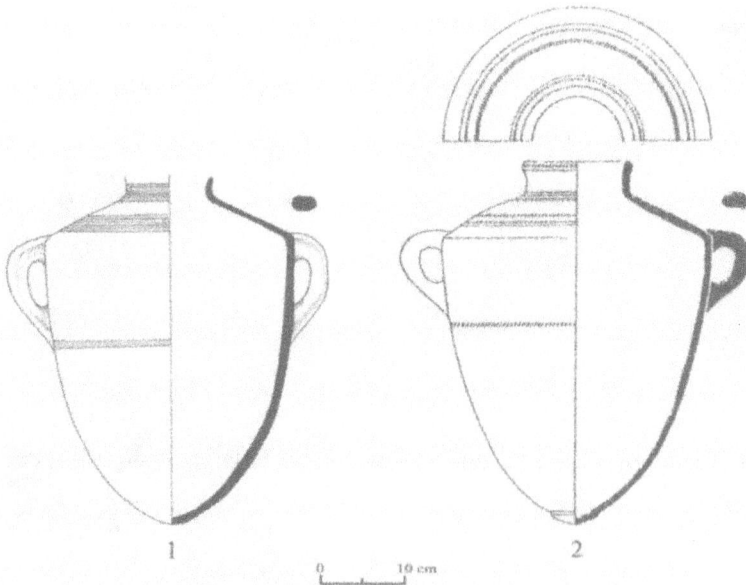

Figure 38. Monochrome decorated jars: 1: Dor; 2: Keisan.

To this group of local imitations of Aegean pottery should apparently be added two types of cooking pots which Harrison recently attributed to a "Philistine" origin. Aside from their presence at most sites of the Northern Sea Peoples mentioned above, Harrison also finds parallels for them at southern Philistine sites, such as Qasile and Ekron (Harrison 2004:30). The present writer tends to agree with him as regards the one-handled cooking pot (cf. now also Killebrew 2000:242-243).

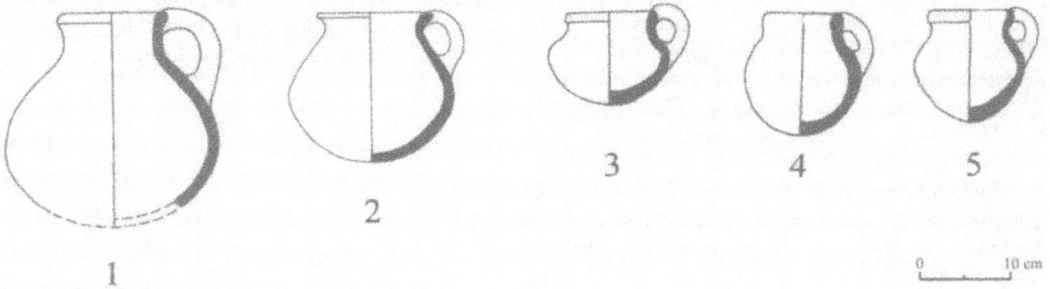

Figure 39. "Philistine" cooking pots from Megiddo VIA.

This was the traditional form of the Aegean cooking pot throughout the ages, but the present writer does not agree with his attribution of an Aegean source for the two-handled jar. However, if Harrison is correct, it is of enormous importance for understanding the process of the Sea Peoples' settling in the area (Fig. 39), even if Yasur-Landdau is correct in regarding them as a hybrid between Aegean and Local Canaanite (Yasur-Landau 2005:180-183).

Among the vessels not found in the southern pottery group are several local types, such as the biconical jug with two handles and a spout, and the biconical jug with one handle without a spout (Fig. 40).

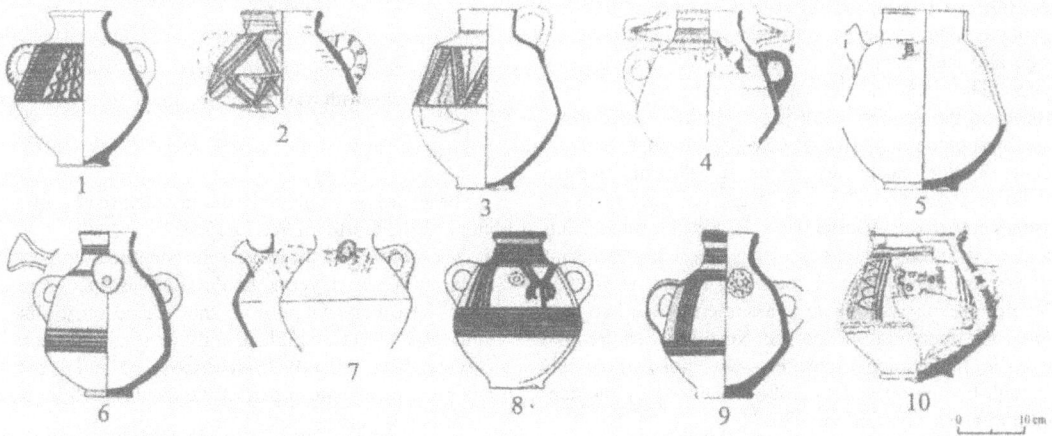

Figure 40. Monochrome decorated jugs with two handles and a spout: 1, 6, 8–9: Megiddo; 2: Dor; 3–4, 10: Keisan; 5: Afula; 7: Yokne'am

All these vessels are decorated in red or red-violet and are unique in their simple horizontal linear design and an occasionally more complex decoration of the western motifs noted above: Antithetical concentric circles, semicircles, metopes, Maltese crosses, net-filled or solid triangles and rhombuses, hourglasses, etc. At times, as in the case of the strainer-spout jug from Megiddo (if it is, indeed, not an imported southern Philistine vessel), depictions appear, apparently of a cultic nature, of a man playing a stringed instrument, a fish, a crab, and several four-legged animals (Fig. 16).

The close resemblance between this group of pottery and the Philistine bichrome ware is indisputable and requires no further explanation—a glance at the comparative plates is sufficient. At the same time, it should be noted that this local pottery assemblage, with its unique red decoration, is more varied in character than the southern ware, and the reason may be that stronger indigenous (Canaanite) elements persisted among the local population in the north, alongside the newcomers, than in the south. However, the difference may also be chronological, since in the north this pottery begins somewhat later and—based on present evidence—does not contain a phase corresponding to the early stage of the Philistine monochrome pottery.

Some scholars also consider the northern monochrome pottery, in whole or in part, as the harbinger of Phoenician bichrome ware: That is, as a Phoenician monochrome phase preceding the Phoenician bichrome ware, and find support for this theory in the finds from Dor (Gilboa 1999a; 1999b; 2009). While it is true that identical pottery types exist in the northern monochrome ware and the Phoenician bichrome, these are only two types: The globular pilgrim flask with round or ring base, and the strainer-spout jugs. All the other Phoenician bichrome types—the ordinary bowls, jugs, and juglets with ridged neck—are exclusively Phoenician types (Amiran 1969:269–271), which are not present in the pottery repertoire described above. On the other hand, none of the other vessel types of northern monochrome pottery are found in the Phoenician bichrome ware. It therefore seems reasonable to assume that the two families—the monochrome of the Northern Sea Peoples and the Phoenician bichrome—developed separately (though both were undoubtedly influenced by the contemporaneous Cypriot pottery).

In this connection we should mention the large pithoi decorated with a wavy relief design of Cypriot origin found in the Sikil strata at Dor (Areas B1 and G and recently also in Area D1, Fig. 41); similar vessels have

also been uncovered at other sites in Palestine from this period. These large vessels were widespread on the island mainly in the Late Bronze Age and their production there ceased almost completely at the beginning of the Iron Age (see detailed discussion of this vessel in Gilboa 2001a, and bibliography there). A. Raban and R. A. Stieglitz suggested several years ago that these vessels were connected with the settlement of the Northern Sea Peoples in Palestine (Raban and Stieglitz 1991: 41–42).

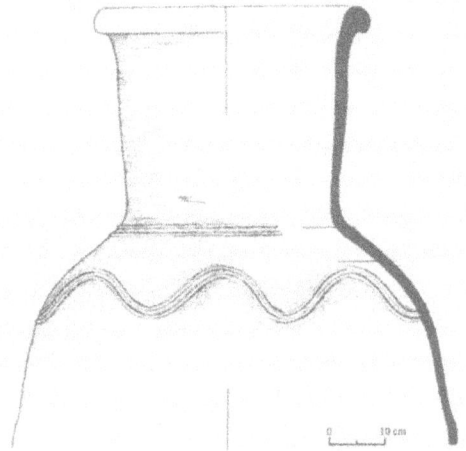

Figure 41. Pithos with wavy relief decoration from Dor, Area B1.

These pithoi exhibit all the characteristics of the pottery of the Northern Sea Peoples:

1. The source of these vessels and their unusual decoration was Cyprus in the Late Bronze Age. They were very common in that period on the island, reached the mainland only in small numbers (several have recently been discovered at Hazor), and perhaps became a part of the local repertoire as early as this period.

2. Just as their production ceased in Cyprus at the beginning of the Iron Age, they began to appear in relatively large numbers and in widespread distribution along the northern coast of Palestine. Important

for our discussion is their discovery in strata from the end of the twelfth and the eleventh centuries BCE at sites such as 'Akko, Tell Keisan, Tell Abu Hawam, and Dor; according to Raban, they are also found at Ashdod in Philistia.

3. Petrographic tests of these vessels (of which many were performed) indicate that they were produced on the northern coast of Palestine (with the exception of perhaps one or two of Cypriot origin). It is possible—as some have proposed (Gilboa 2001a:169-170; Sherratt 1998)—that these vessels were produced by Cypriot potters working on the coast of Palestine; it is generally believed that these very large vessels were not transported commercially. In my opinion however, if we take into account the background of all the pottery finds enumerated above, these vessels can in fact corroborate the theory of Raban and Stieglitz that they were produced through the influence of the Sea Peoples who migrated from Cyprus and settled in the north of the country.

4
CULT OBJECTS

INTRODUCTION

We will turn now to another aspect of the material culture of the Sikils and other northern Sea Peoples that has been extensively dealt with in the past by T. Dothan and A. Mazar—the unique cult of the Sea Peoples (T. Dothan 1982; 2003b; A. Mazar 1980; 1985a; 2000; Stern 1991; 2000b; 2006; Ben-Shlomo and Press 2009; Press 2012). We shall examine the objects of this cult, which appear together with the pottery, compare them with similar finds from Cyprus and Philistia, and attempt to determine whether the cult finds of the northern tribes differ from, or are similar to, those of the Philistines.

The cult finds we have attributed to the Sikil inhabitants of Dor, or to the other cities of the Northern Sea Peoples, consist of no fewer than ten different types. At Dor, some of them were uncovered in a definite Sikil stratum. Others, although unstratified, exhibit the well-known Aegean-Cypriot cultic tradition. These objects include: Clay anthropomorphic vessels and figurines, bull-shaped clay libation vessels, bulls depicted on ivory plaques and gold jewelry, clay "wall brackets" including brackets with painted bulls or in relief, clay lioness-headed cups, clay stands, bone scapulae, and seals.

We shall begin our discussion with the anthropomorphic vessels and figurines.

CLAY ANTHROPOMORPHIC VESSELS AND FIGURINES

Due to their distinctive features, two types of anthropomorphic cultic finds from Dor and the other northern sites are attributed to the Sea Peoples tradition: One, an anthropomorphic juglet, was first uncovered by A. Mazar in a Philistine sanctuary in Stratum XII at Tell Qasile (Fig. 42:2). It was described by him as follows:

> The juglet has a pear-shaped body, plain round base, and a handle. It was probably wheel-made, but during the molding of the human face, when the vessel was leather-hard, the body was slightly squashed. The face was shaped on the neck of the vessel by applying additional clay. The face has a long protruding nose, eyes in the form of coffee-beans, large, protruding ears and a short, rectangular beard (or protruding chin?). The eyebrows are emphasized by two minute pieces of clay and above them is a long clay coil, passing across the forehead and curving behind the ears. This coil may represent the hair-do or more likely, two rams' horns. The possible rams' horns may point to an identification of the figure as a male god. (A. Mazar 1980:81–82, Fig. 19, Pl. 30)

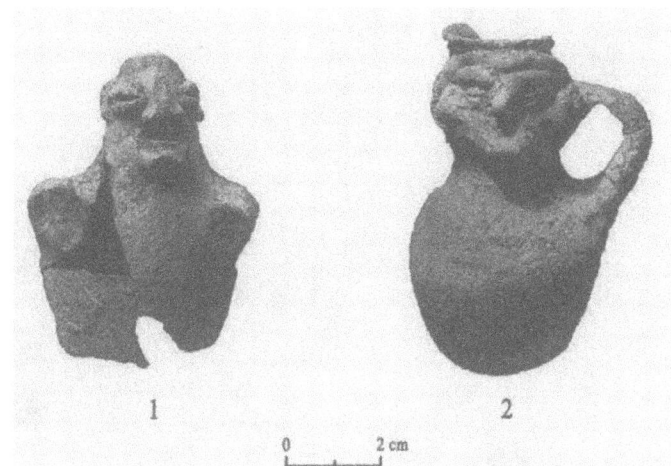

Figure. 42. Local anthropomorphic juglets connected with Sea Peoples cult: 1: Dor; 2: Tell Qasile.

The northern example, which comes from Dor (Fig. 42:1), is an anthropomorphic juglet similar to the one from Qasile, and depicts a human male figure with slanted, coffee-bean shaped eyes.

Although not found complete, it came from Area D2, in a stratum definitely belonging to the Sikils (Stern 2000a:347, Fig. 245). As this type of object has been found thus far in Israel nowhere else but in Philistine and Sikil sites and strata, we may assume that both objects belong to the Sea Peoples, and probably to the northern ones, as they are by now found only in the area from the Yarkon river and north of it.

The second anthropomorphic type, the clay figurine, is known from sites that were probably settled in this period by the Northern Sea Peoples. One figurine (of which only the head was preserved) was found many years ago by M. Dothan in Stratum IIIA in the mound of Afula, not far from Megiddo in the center of the Jezreel Valley, together with many "Philistine" pottery vessels, i.e., typical pottery of the Northern Sea Peoples (here

Fig. 43:5; and see above). The features of this figurine indicate a connection with the peculiar Cypro-Philistine cult (M. Dothan 1957:141–142, Fig. 15:19, Pl. VI:1).

This type of figurine was quite common during the Iron Age I in southern Palestine, and was found at almost every Philistine site: They were uncovered in large numbers at Ashdod (Dothan and Freedman 1967:162–163, Fig. 163:1–3; M. Dothan 1971:141, Fig. 65; Pl. LV; here Fig. 43:2, 10); Ashkelon (Stager 2001:75; Ben Shelomo and Press 2009; Press 2012); Tell Jemmeh (Van-Beek 1993:669); and Ekron (cf. Dothan and Ben-Shlomo 2005:180-186; 243-245; Ben-Shlomo and Press 2009), and up to the Yarkon river (Guzowska and Yasur-Landou 2009:392-393; Ben Shlomo and Press 2009).

A figurine found at Tel Batash (Panitz-Cohen and Mazar 2006:253; Photo 107) was called by A. Mazar the "Cyrano Head" (here, too, only the head was found), and he claimed that "this figurine retains the Aegean and Cypriot tradition" (here Fig. 44).

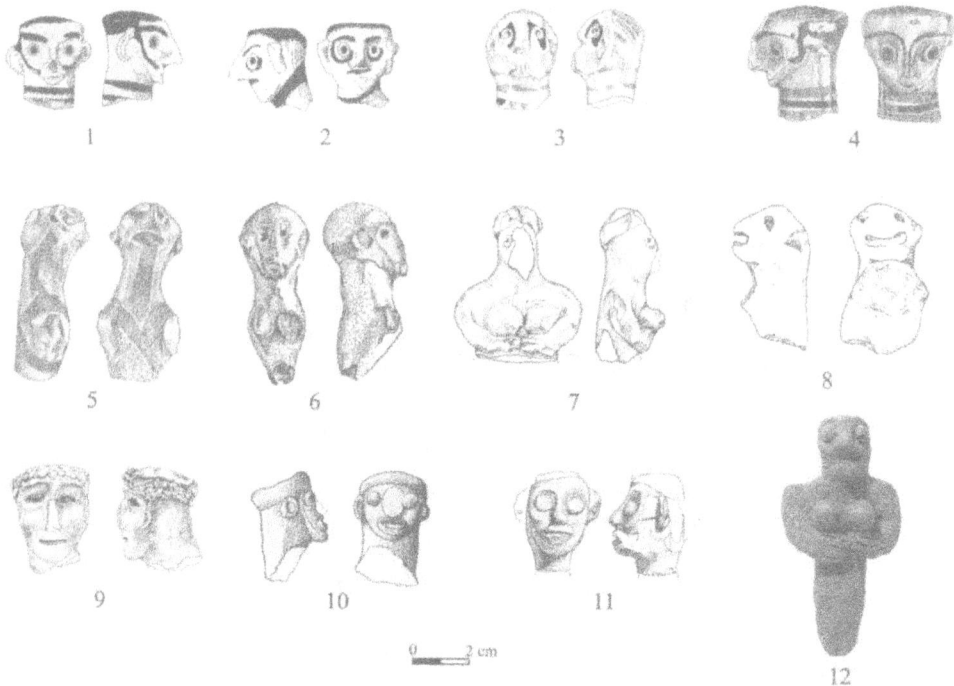

Figure. 43. "Sea Peoples" figurines from: 1: Cyprus (Enkomi); 2: Ashdod; 3: Beth-Shean; 4:Yokne'am; 5: Afula; 6: Kh. Sitt Leila; 7: Beth-Shean; 8: Megiddo; 9: Beth Shean; 10: Ashdod; 11: Tell Keisan; 12: Tel Gerisa.

Figure 44. "Cyrano Head" from Tel Batash.

M. Dothan, too, in his detailed discussion of the Afu-la figurine (Dothan 1955), attributed it to Mycenaean and Cypriot prototypes, and indeed quite a few similar figurines were found in Enkomi (Fig. 43:1) and other sites on the island (Karageorghis 1993:Pls. XVII:1; XVIII–XIX). It seems now that the "Cyrano-Head" figurines, many of which were uncovered in a Philistine context in the south and at sites of the Sea Peoples in the north, were executed according to the same Cypriot tradition and in Palestine are characteristic of all Sea People sites.

Figurines similar to the Afula head were uncov-ered in other northern sites, which also included typi-cal pottery. A fine example of a female figurine of clay was discovered by Z. Herzog in the Philistine levels of Tel Gerisa (Fig. 43:12; Herzog 1993:483).

A third one was discovered at Tell Keisan in the 1930s by a British team (Fig. 43:11), but was published only much later, and not in its proper context, in the French final report (Briend and Humbert 1980:Pl. 102:1), and another was found recently at Yokne'am (Ben-Tor 1993:810; here Fig. 43:4). A fifth was uncovered many years ago in a survey conducted by Y. Aharoni at Khirbet Sitt Leila in Mount Carmel, just a few kilometers south-east of Dor (Aharoni 1958:138, Fig. 1; here Fig. 43:6). Aharoni evidently associated it with the Afula figurine and dated it also to Iron Age I. Similar figurines are known now from Beth-Shean (Panitz-Cohen and Mazar 2009:534-538; here Fig. 43:3, 7 and 9), and another from Yadin's excavations at Megiddo (Zarzecki-Peleg 2005:Fig. 42:13; here Fig. 43:8) as well as one from a

previous dig (May 1935:Pl.xxix no.5029).

It should be added that A. Mazar, who recently pub-lished the three figurines from Beth-Shean, compared them to many other examples, all of them in Philistia: From Ashdod, Ashkelon, Ekron, Tell eş-Şâfi/Gath and Tel Batash (Panitz-Cohen and Mazar 2009:534-538; and cf. Ben-Shlomo and Press 2009; compare especial-ly our Fig. 43 with Ben-Shlomo and Press 2009:55, Fig. 10 and 58, Fig 15).

BULL-SHAPED CLAY LIBATION VESSELS

Of the second type of cult object, the bull-shaped clay libation vessel, one (with the head missing) was found at Dor in a Sikil stratum in Area D2. The vessel, which was produced locally, bears a red–purple painted net decoration in a typical Cypriot monochrome design (Fig. 45:3). This vessel can be compared with an almost identical bull vessel from Tell Abu Hawam (Fig. 45:2) ascribed to one of the Stratum V phases, probably the late one (Hamilton 1935:Fig. 248); it, too, is decorated with a red net pattern.

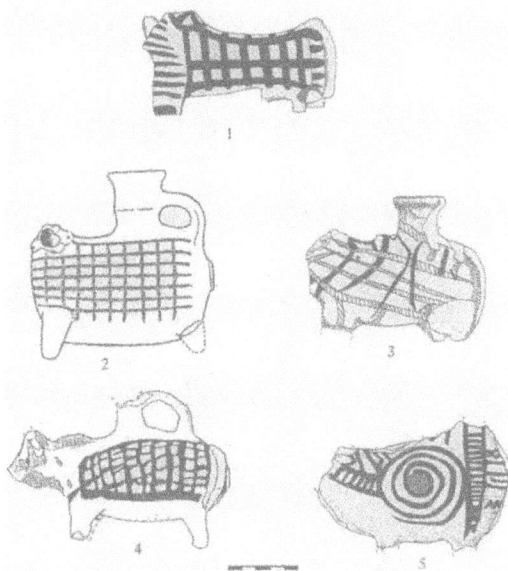

Figure 45. Bull-shaped clay libation vessels: 1: Cyprus; 2: Tell Abu Hawam; 3: Dor; 4-5: Ekron.

Numerous clay bull libation vessels found at Ekron (Fig. 45:4–5) in the various Philistine strata (Strata VII and V; Ben-Shlomo 1999:17–19, Pls. 1–2; 2008a:27; Fig. 2:2) resemble the Dor and Tell Abu Hawam finds. Some of the Ekron examples are decorated with the same red monochrome net pattern as the one from Dor (and cf. Fig. 45:3), but others bear the typical Philistine bichrome spiral motif (Fig. 45:5; Ben-Shlomo 1999, Fig. 13; Ben-Shlomo 2008a:27; Fig. 2:1). There can be no doubt that all these bull libation vessels which served as cultic objects had been inspired by earlier Mycenaean and later Cypriot prototypes, which continued to be produced locally during the early Iron Age (Yon 1994: 190–191, Fig. 41:1).

We should also mention that bull figurines continued to play an important role in the Philistine cult even until the ninth century BCE, as is proved perhaps by their frequent appearance among the clay stands of the Yavneh favissa (Ziffer-Kletter 2007:38-46).

IVORY BULL PLAQUES

This plaque, probably also of Cypriot origin, depicts a cult scene featuring the Aegean bull; it was uncovered at Tel Dor in Area B1 on the eastern side of the mound and probably belongs to Stratum 10. The plaque, made of bone or ivory, may have originally adorned a wooden box, and indeed additional parts of a similar plaque was also recovered. It was carved with the well-known Cypriot scene of a bull goring a lotus flower (Fig. 46:1).

This find is not unique in Palestine. It resembles an ivory handle or cosmetic box depicting the "goring bull" motif found at Megiddo in Stratum VIA (Loud 1948:Pl. 204 3; Harrison 2004:Pl.28:7 and see here Fig. 46:3). Another ivory lid comes from Ekron, where it was found in Area IV in an administrative center together with Philistine bichrome ware.

T. Dothan dated it to the last quarter of the twelfth century BCE or the beginning of the eleventh. It is decorated "with an unmistakably Aegean style depicting battles between various animals including bulls, griffin and lions in a circle" (Dothan and Gitin 1994:13–14; here Fig. 46:4; T. Dothan 2006). T. Dothan also believes that

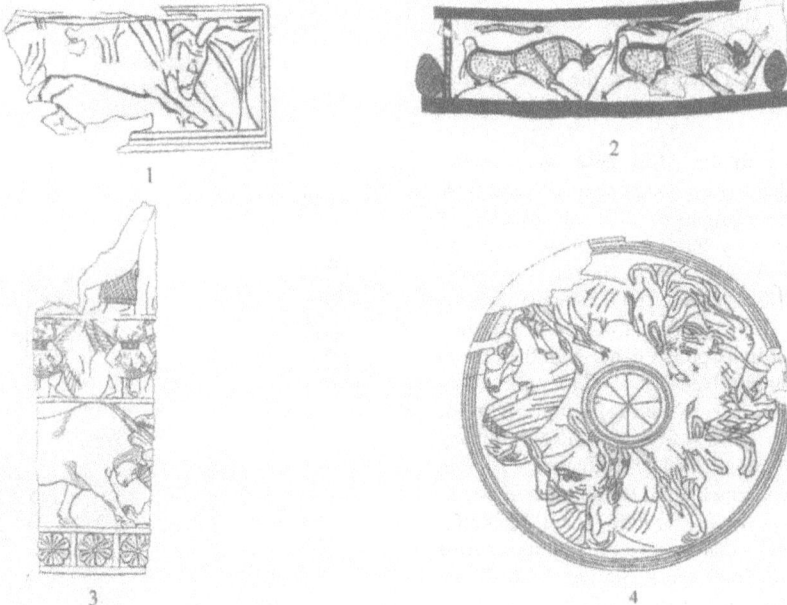

Figure 46. Ivory bull carvings: 1: Dor; 2: Cyprus; 3: Megiddo VI; 4: Ekron

"the closest parallels to the ivory lid from Ekron are the incised lids from Palaepaphos, Cyprus, which resembles the Ekron lid in terms of the decorative theme, combination of motifs and design. The animal battle is a typical motif in western art, and presumably reached Cyprus via Crete. The animal's vigorous and assertive character is based on Aegean prototypes" (T. Dothan 2006).

The plaques with the bull motif from Dor, Megiddo, and Ekron represent only a small part of an increasingly large assemblage of ivories from the Iron Age I (Ben-Shlomo and Dothan 2006; T. Dothan 2006; and see bibliography there).

Figure 47. Cypriot clay jug depicting a "goring bull and a flower" (c. 25 cm high).

A bull goring a flower is a typical Cypriot motif and also appears in Cyprus on scores of pottery vessels and other objects from various periods, and reached its floruit in the Iron Age (Fig. 46:2; Fig. 47). The goring bull motif, or the bull as a participant in various cult ceremonies, was very common in Mycenaean art of the Late Bronze Age and even earlier, and after arriving in Cyprus it became popular at first among the Sea Peoples, and later also among the local population (Yon 1994:193). The plaques decorated with a Cypriot scene found at Dor and Megiddo should probably also be attributed to the local Sea Peoples.

GOLD BULL EARRINGS AND JEWELRY

Another image of a bull on a piece of gold jewelry (perhaps one of a pair of earrings, see here Fig. 48) was uncovered at Dor in Area D2 in Stratum 10, which dates to the end of the eleventh century BCE. It is not certain that the earring was found in situ and it may have survived from an earlier stratum. There is no doubt that this earring is also of Cypriot style, and was produced either in Cyprus or in Palestine.

In Cyprus itself a number of similar pieces of gold jewelry depicting the heads of bulls were discovered, both from earlier periods and contemporaneous with our find. (For a number of bull heads from Enkomi and Kition, see Pieridou 1971:Pl. IX:1–3).

I sent a photograph of the earring to Professor Vassos Karageorghis, who informed me (on March 2, 2004) that this type of jewelry was common in Cyprus during the Late Cypriot period, which corresponds chronologically to our Iron Age I, but it was not produced in Cyprus, as all Cypriot examples he was familiar with were made in repoussé or granulation, while ours is plain. He therefore believes that our earring must have been a local imitation of a Cypriot prototype (cf. Åström 1972:502, Groups 6 and 7; Pieridou 1971:Pl. IX:1).

The role of the bull in the Cypriot-Aegean cult and in that of the Sea Peoples in this period can be learned not only from its depiction on libation vessels, bone plaques and gold jewelry, all of which have been found at Dor, but also from its frequent appearance on the clay "wall brackets" in the settlements of the Sea Peoples (mainly in the north) in Palestine and, of course, in Cyprus (see below).

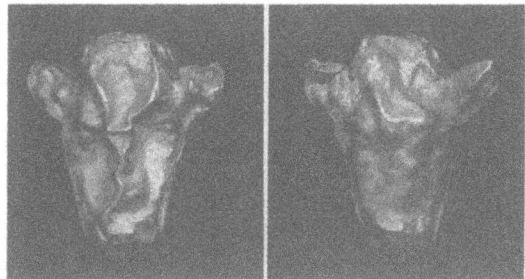

Figure 48. Bull-shaped gold earring from Dor (c. 1.5 cm high).

We discussed above only one type of jewelry but there were certainly many others, among them in particular are the earrings called "earplugs". These kinds of earrings have been found up to now in two sites in Israel in the eleventh century BCE contexts. The first three were uncovered in Tel Miqne (Philistine Ekron; T. Dothan 1998; 2003a). Two of them are made of ivory and one of faience. One other, made of glass, was found in Dor, Area G, also in Iron Age I contexts (Zorn and Brill 2007; here Fig. 49).

There can be no doubt that the source of these artifacts is Egyptian, as had been proved by T. Dothan (cf. T. Dothan 1998; 2003a), but in Palestine they were in exclusive use by the Sea Peoples as is evidenced by the sites where they were found: Ekron and Dor. Zorn and Brill, who published the glass earplug from Dor, came to the same conclusions: "It is intriguing to note the cultural connection between Dor and Ekron: Both sites were settled by groups of Sea Peoples" (Zorn and Brill 2007:257).

In addition to the two types of earrings there are probably more jewelry types used exclusively by the Sea Peoples, both the Philistines in the south and the Northern Sea Peoples, but these are beyond the scope of this presentation.

WALL BRACKETS

The last group of Cypriot-type bulls dating to the beginning of the Iron Age to be discussed here appears on reliefs or drawings on clay wall-brackets which, despite

Figure 49. Earplugs: 1: Dor (Glass), 2: Ekron (Faience).

their Cypriot origin, were produced almost exclusively in Palestine. At Dor only a small fragment of this type of wall bracket was found, not in situ; its exact function has not yet been conclusively established. Many finds of this type, however, have been uncovered in settlements of the Northern Sea Peoples from the twelfth and eleventh centuries BCE.

Original Cypriot wall brackets, to which painted ap-

Figure 50. "Wall brackets": 1–3: Cypriot; 4: Megiddo VI.

pliqué decorations representing a protome of a bull were attached, have been uncovered at numerous sites in Cyprus (Fig. 50:1–3; cf. Karageorghis 2006), most of them from the Late Bronze Age; a small number have also been attributed to the beginning of the Iron Age (Åström 1972; Yon 1994; Schlipphak 2001). Cypriot wall brackets with painted bull decorations have also been found (Fig. 50:4, and cf. Panitz-Cohen 2003; 2006).

The "wall bracket" is essentially a Cypriot cult object. It has been found up till now in large numbers in both Cyprus and Palestine from the Late Bronze Age. It disappears almost completely in Cyprus and in Israel after the Iron Age Ib (eleventh century BCE).

The most important site for the clay wall-brackets within the area under discussion is without doubt Megiddo. No less than eleven objects of this type have been found there, all of them dating to strata of the Iron Age IB: Stratum VI and VIA. They include one bracket from Schumacher's excavations and another from Yadin's. A fragment of another bracket was discovered in a tomb (and see Harrison 2004:Pl. 24).

According to Panitz-Cohen (2006:625), the data from Megiddo indicate that the chronological framework is mainly Iron IB, Stratum VI, and that most of the motifs are unique to Megiddo. Even those that have parallels in the Cypriot and Levantine contexts in LB IIB and LC III have deviant details of execution and iconography that fit their local and later manufacture. Of the four brackets examined petrographically, three are locally made, and one was manufactured somewhere on the north-

ern coast between the Carmel and Sarepta. Most of the wall brackets from Megiddo included various religious symbols, engraved painted or in relief, including bulls' heads (Fig. 50:4).

All the other Iron Age I wall brackets came from four northern sites and only two from southern sites: Beth-Shean (Strata VII and Lower VI), Yokne'am (Stratum XVII), Tell Keisan (Stratum 9C), and, as was mentioned above, a small fragment was found at Dor in an unstratified context (not yet published).

Of the two wall brackets discovered in the south, one comes from Tel Gerisa (not yet published) and the other from Ashdod—in both cases in Philistine contexts. From the interior of the country, only two fragments of wall brackets are known so far: One from the City of David and the other from Lachish; their dates, however, are uncertain and both of them may belong to the Late Bronze Age.

It should also be noted that the attribution of these objects to the Sea Peoples is corroborated by—aside from their definite Cypriot origin—the finds from Megiddo where at least two were found together with classic "Philistine" pottery of Stratum VIB. According to Panitz-Cohen, two of the loci in which these objects were uncovered belong to a square in which were also found a "Philistine" bowl, kraters, a jug and a double bronze axe of the usual Sea Peoples type (Fig. 51 and 61:1-2).

It thus appears that these wall brackets are the remains of a cultic assemblage belonging to the Sea Peoples. Another bracket from Megiddo was also found alongside the famous Philistine strainer-spout jug bearing the

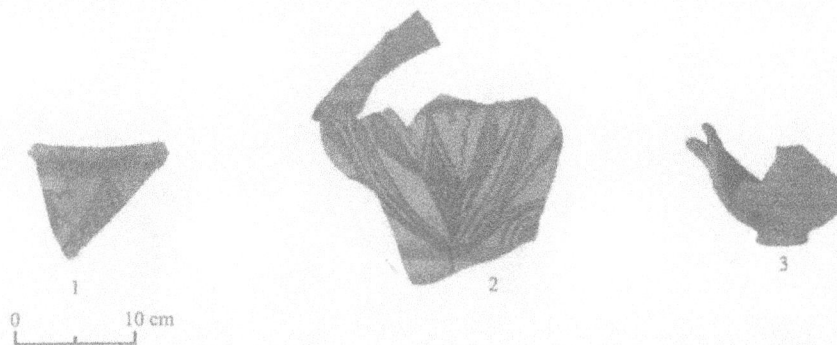

1   0   10 cm   2   3

Figure 51. "Philistine" pottery from Megiddo VIB found with a "wall bracket" and bronze ax (see here, Figs. 46:4 and 57; Loud 1948, Pls.142:7, 11–12; 183:14)

Orpheus decoration described above (see here Fig. 16).

In summarizing the wall brackets, we may quote again the conclusions of Panitz-Cohen:

> The argument . . . is that the bracket is a purely Cypriot cultic object and that its arrival in the east was initially the result of personal import on the part of the Cypriot "trading diaspora" (Sherratt and Sherratt 1991:354) or possibly Cypriot craftsmen (metalworkers or potters?) residing on the Levantine coast. While emulation and imitation may have subsequently occurred, its primary symbolic essence remained meaningful for the Cypriots alone. Since we find this object at two sites in the east [Megiddo and Beth-Shean] that did not contain them before the twelfth century BCE, it may be assumed that its local production at this time was not the result of emulation or imitation but was rather to serve the specific religious needs of some local inhabitants. Thus, it seems that the owners of these brackets must have been Cypriots residing at Beth–Shean and Megiddo. (Panitz-Cohen 2006:625)

Now, if we change here the "Cypriots" into "Northern Sea Peoples"—as the present writer thinks it should be—it will fit all other locally made "Cypriot" finds discussed in this presentation.

CLAY LIONESS-HEADED CUPS

One of the cult objects long attributed to the Philistines is the clay lioness-headed cup. T. Dothan, in her comprehensive study, discussed all the finds uncovered in Israel up to 1982 (T. Dothan 1982:229–234, and see detailed bibliography there). She studied five lion-headed cups that bore all the hallmarks of the Philistine decorative style, uncovered at Tel Zeror, Tell eş-Şâfi/Gath, Megiddo, Tel Gerisa, and Tell Qasile. These cups are one-handled drinking or libation cups that have no opening in the mouth (an unusual feature for this type of vessel).

Stylistically, T. Dothan divided them into two groups:

Group A. The cups from Tel Zeror, Megiddo, and Tell eş-Şâfi/Gath with closed mouths and naturalistic, delicately rendered features.

Group B. The less naturalistic, cruder cups from Tel Gerisa and Tell Qasile with open jaws showing tongue and fangs, bulging eyes and cheeks, flat-

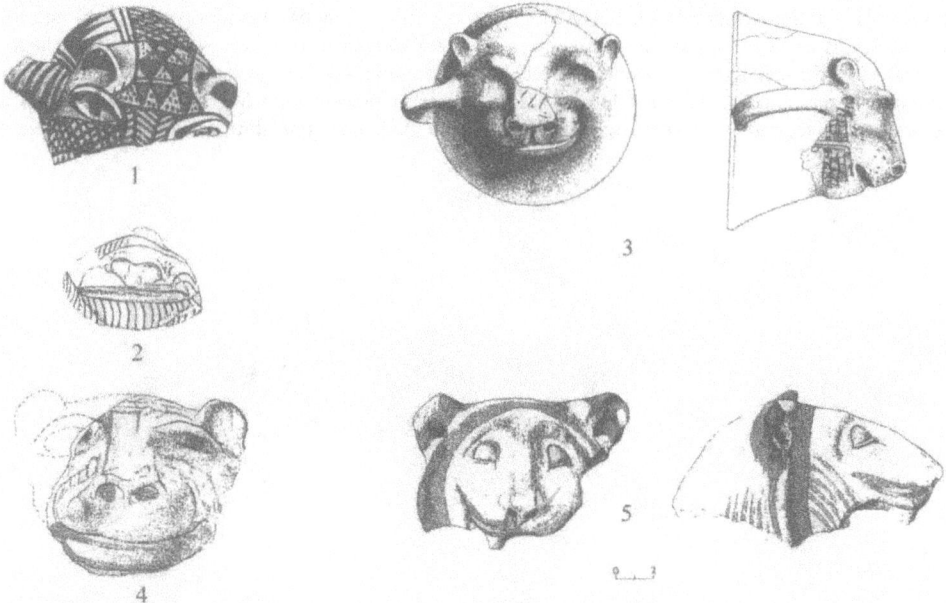

Figure 52. Lioness-headed cups: 1: Megiddo; 2: Dor; 3: Tel Zeror; 4: Tell eş-Şâfi/Gath; 5: Ashdod.

tened noses, and upturned muzzles.

The cups of both groups were decorated with painted designs that accentuate the features (red and black on a whitish slip) and filling ornaments that do not convey the surface texture of a real animal but correspond to the planes of the face.

T. Dothan concluded that the Philistine pottery cups seemed to have had the same raison d'être as those of the Mycenaeans—they were an inexpensive substitute for silver, gold, and stone vessels. They were part of the widely distributed *koine* artifacts of Mycenaean IIIB. The majority, decorated in the style of Mycenean pottery, were found in Cyprus and Ugarit. Yet among all these animal-headed cups there was not a single example of a lioness's head in Mycenaean ware and decoration, although plain examples are known from Thera and Ugarit. No animal-headed cups have so far been found in Mycenaean IIIC pottery. Thus the group of Philistine lioness-headed cups evidently continued the Mycenaean IIIB zoomorphic cup tradition and filled a gap in the corpus of animal-headed pottery cups.

However, it seems now to the writer that these Sea Peoples' vessels of the early Iron Age continue, in a cheaper material, the Cypriot Late Bronze faience cups in the shape of lioness, ram or even female heads found in Israel at Tell Abu Hawam and recently also at Hazor (but cf. Zuckerman 2008 and bibliography there).

Since Dothan's study of these cups, some additional clay lioness-headed cups have been found, five in the Philistine Pentapolis: One at Ashdod (Dothan and Porath 1982:136–137, Fig. 18; and here Fig. 52:5); the second at Tell eṣ-Ṣâfi/Gath, in addition to previous ones found there long ago (see here Fig. 52:4; and Maeir and Ehrlich 2001:29; Maeir 2006); three at Ekron (Dothan-Gitin 1990:Front page; Ben-Shlomo 2008:34-35; Fig. 8); and a sixth at Dor (Stern 2000a:94–96, Fig 48; here Fig. 52:2). The Dor find consists of a fragment of a cup in the form of the head of a lioness decorated with painted patterns of a type found at the other Philistine sites. It was not found in a stratigraphic context, but it was easy to identify and attribute to this group. It bears a "Philistine" bichrome painted decoration and closely resembles the older cups found at Tell eṣ-Ṣâfi/Gath (compare Fig. 52:2 and Fig. 52:4).

To sum up, all the lioness-headed cups found in the southern part of the country came from only well-known Philistine cities such as Ashdod, Ekron, Tell eṣ-Ṣâfi/Gath, Tell Qasile and Tel Gerisa. In the northern part of the country, i.e., the territory of the Northern Sea Peoples, three were found: One from Tel Zeror (Fig. 52:3);

one from Tel Dor; and one from Megiddo (Fig. 52:1). There are no marked differences between the cups from the south and the north, and all seem to have been executed according to the same western, mainly Cypriot, tradition.

In this context the biblical story of Samson and the lion (Judges 14:1–9) should be noted, as well as the find of an almost complete lion's skull in a sanctuary at Jaffa, which was dated by its excavator, J. Kaplan, to the early Iron Age and attributed to the Philistines (Kaplan and Ritter-Kaplan 1993:656). But according to Gadot (Gadot 2008:60), Z. Herzog, the later excavator of Jaffa, informed him that the date of the temple should be raised to the fourteenth century BCE and above it there was even another stratum belonging to the period of Ramesses II. But knowing Kaplan's method of working, it is very hard for me to believe that he was unable to distinguish between Late Bronze and early Iron Age strata.

A. Mazar, in his discussion of the complete lion-headed cup and the additional fragments from Tell Qasile (A. Mazar 1980:101–103), claimed that the animal-shaped cups may have been intended for use either as cult vessels or as elaborate secular vessels which could also be used for cult purposes. The latter explanation was suggested by M. P. Nilsson and others in their studies of the elaborate rhytons of the Aegean world (Nilsson 1950: 145; Koehl 2006).

Other scholars, however, have proposed different interpretations of these vessels and their significance in the Philistine cult; see now the summary in Maeir 2006: 340–342, in which he describes an additional cup discovered in his excavations at Tell eṣ-Ṣâfi/Gath (see also Ben-Shlomo 2008a:34-35).

Figure 53. The cup from Nahal Patish (diameter c. 12 cm).

In 2008, an additional lioness cup, the most complete and beautiful ever found in Israel, came to light
in a Philistine temple excavated in Nahal Patish near
Mishmar Hanegev in the western Negev. This cup
was uncovered together with other Philistine cult objects of the type found in the Tell Qasile sanctuaries –
stands, chalices, and bowls decorated in Philistine style
(Nahshoni 2009:92; here, Fig 53). Up to now at least
three of the cups were found in temple contexts, one
in Qasile Stratum XI, one at Ekron, and one at Nahal
Patish; another one (from Tel Zeror) was found in a
cemetery.

The importance of lions and lionesses in the
Philistine cult until even the tenth and ninth centuries BCE. is attested now by their frequent presence in
the Philistine favissa of this age at Yavneh (Ziffer and
Kletter 2007:28-34; Kletter, Ziffer, and Zwickel 2010:
pls. 18, 20).

CLAY STANDS

In the northern part of Area G at Tel Dor, remains of
a building were found in one of the Sikil phases. Discovered in a relatively limited area, it was impossible
to establish the complete plan of the structure. Among
its remains was found a group of about a dozen pottery
vessels, mostly offering bowls, near a bench attached to
one of the walls. Included in this cache were two cultic
vessels typical of the Sea Peoples:

1. A ceramic incense burner on a square stand with
human figures, executed in an unusual cut-out technique (Fig. 54:1). Similar cultic vessels have been
found in the Philistine temples at Tell Qasile (Fig
54:2) and Ashdod.
2. A clay chalice decorated with a red stripe and
with two horizontal handles on both sides (Stern
2000a: 96, Fig 47; Mazar 1980:87–89, Fig. 23, Pl.
32; M. Dothan in Stern 1993:29).

While the chalice with its horizontal handles is undoubtedly a typical product of the Sea Peoples tradition,
the stand is a rare find, especially in its unusual technique. Similar clay stands have been found up to now
only in Philistine assemblages.

The first parallel comes from Tell Qasile, where it was
found in the Philistine sanctuary No. 131. A. Mazar described it thus:

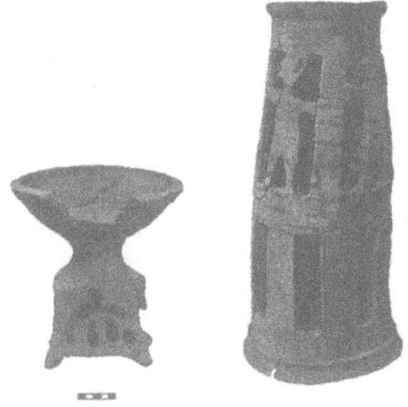

Figure 54. Clay stands: 1:Dor; 2: Qasile.

The stand was wheel-made as a cylinder, open at either
end, with an everted, rounded rim. When leather hard,
two rows of windows were cut in its walls. The lower row
has seven rectangular windows and horizontal grooves
delineate the upper and lower borders of the spaces between the windows. The upper row includes four trap-
ezoidal windows. In each of the windows a schematic
human figure is shown striding with outstretched hands,
the head in profile. The figures were formed by cut-
ting out the windows around the contour lines in *ajouré*
(open work) technique; they are thus an integral part of
the vessel fabric (A. Mazar 1980: 87–89, Fig. 23, Pl. 32).

The difference between the stand from Qasile and
that of Dor is that in the former the human figures were
executed by contour lines while those from Dor were
cut out and depicted in the hollows.

In his discussion of the Qasile stand, A. Mazar brought
analogies, of which the most important is the so-called
"musicians' stand" from Stratum X at Ashdod (T. Dothan 1982:249–250; Dothan and Ben-Shlomo 2005:245-
247). He concluded that both the Qasile stand and the
Ashdod stand depicted parts of a ritual scene which, to
his mind, belonged to the Philistines and originated in
Cyprus. "Though the stands differ from one another,
we may conclude that the above-mentioned group of
cult stands from Palestine represents a specific artistic
trend which developed in the eleventh century BCE along
the coast and the Jezre'el plain" (A. Mazar 1980:250).

I concur with this opinion and also believe that both
the chalice and the stand from Dor should be interpret-
ed as cultic vessels which were in use by the local Sea
Peoples.

COW SCAPULAE

Another cultic object, probably also connected with the Sea Peoples and originating in Cyprus, is the cow scapula, or shoulder blade, which is recognized by the incisions cut in parallel lines along its upper edge. It was probably used to divine a message from a god. The purpose of the notches is uncertain. It has also been suggested that the incisions were made to produce a musical sound when the bone was waved in the air or when another object, perhaps a stick, stroked it. Others suggest (Webb 1985; Karageorghis 1990; and recent detailed discussion in Zukerman 2007:69-73) that they were used in prognostication, which seems more plausible.

In the northern part of the country, they have been found aside from Tel Dor, also at Kabri, Tell Abu Hawam, Tel Kinrot, Megiddo and Ta'anach (Zukerman 2007:65-69). At Tel Dor, fragments of at least three different scapulae were found, none in a clear stratigraphic context (here, Fig. 55:1; Stern 2000a:99, Fig. 49).

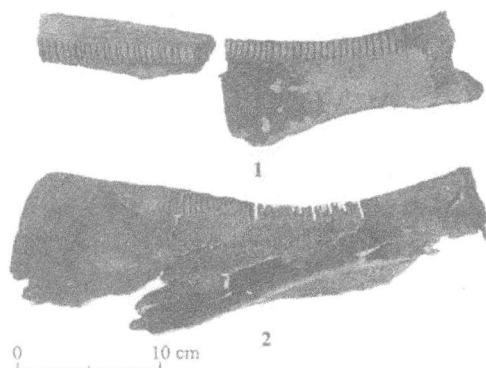

Figure 55. Cow scapulae: 1: Dor; 2: Ekron.

All the others were uncovered only in Philistine cities: Ashkelon, Tell eṣ-Ṣâfi/Gath, and Ekron (here, Fig. 55:2). In Ekron no fewer then seventeen of these incised shoulder blades were discovered, eleven of which dated to the Iron Age I and four to the Iron Age II (the others unstratified, those from Iron Age I, come from all Philistine Strata VI to IVA). In the Philistine shrines they were probably associated with the local ritual of divination in which the god delivers a message or gives advice. T. Dothan noted that the earliest scapula at Ekron

was found in Stratum VI, which may mark this shrine as one of the first cultic installations of the Sea Peoples/Philistines established in Philistia (Dothan and Gitin 1990:28; Dothan and Drenka 2009).

Others come from a cultic center of Stratum V, with the largest concentration found in Area I. From Ashkelon only one scapula has been published so far (King and Stager 2001:297); it is attributed by the excavator to the Iron Age I, i.e., to the Philistine town. Four additional scapula fragments were recently found in Tell eṣ-Ṣâfi/Gath, dated by the excavators as late as the ninth century BCE (Zukerman et al 2007) but also considered Philistine.

The majority of these objects, however, were found in Cyprus, especially in the contemporary Kition sanctuaries. The votive material associated with the sacred building in Area II at Kition included no fewer than twelve fragmentary scapulas, carved with the same series of parallel incisions or notches along the posterior border of the ventral face. Both right– and left–hand scapulae are found, though the former occur more frequently. In each case, the incised area has been polished along the length of the bone, subsequent to the completion of the carving. The scapulae were recovered from *bothroi* deposits associated with Temples 4 and 5, a well deposit associated with Temple 4, and floor deposits in Temples 1, 4, and 5. Their stratigraphical contexts range in date from Late Cypriot IIIA through the Geometric, Archaic, and Classical periods (Webb 1985:316–328). Many others have been found in various other Cypriot sites (and see map in Zukerman et al. 2007:58).

T. Dothan therefore concluded that the shoulder blades of Stratum VI at Ekron were of a type familiar from shrines in Cyprus, indicating that this Ekron shrine was one of the first built by the Sea Peoples/Philistines after their journey across the Mediterranean from Cyprus to Canaan. Recently, a catalogue, enumerating all the known cow blades from all periods and regions, was published by D. S. Reese (2002; 2009) and Zukerman (Zukerman et al. 2007).

THE CYLINDER SEAL

Another Cypriot/Sea People object from Dor to be included here is a cylinder seal that was found not in situ in Area B on the eastern side of the mound (Fig. 56). On its discovery, we immediately realized that it was also of Cypriot origin, and at first dated it to the Late

Bronze Age (compare Porada 1948; A. Mazar 1978:13). However, when all the surrounding area for a distance of a few hundred meters failed to produce any finds earlier than the twelfth century BCE, we attributed the seal to this century (or even the early part of the eleventh). In response to a photo of the seal we sent to Joanna S. Smith of Columbia University, an expert in this type of seal, she wrote:

> It is most definitely a late Cypriot piece. It is part of a group of seals often called "common style" so termed because of their rudimentary carving. Both the drill and graver were used, but not in as complex a fashion as on other cylinder seals from Cyprus. This "common style" group is interesting also because their designs may be abbreviated in terms of figural detail, but they are unlike all the other seals in not having a straight-forward linear and fairly two-dimensional arrangement. The orientation of figures, animals, and symbols appear on first glance to be random. On closer inspection, they contain interesting spatial relationships not found in other seal designs of the period. As for the particular Tel Dor seal, it is one that has several parallels among seals from Enkomi, Hala-Sultan-Tekke, and several other sites, and rests comfortably among seals of the thirteenth and the twelfth centuries BCE (Late Cypriot IIC to IIIA periods). While the twelfth century is termed Iron Age I in Israel, Cypriot scholars do not begin using the Iron Age terminology until the late eleventh and tenth centuries BCE.

We should also mention the discovery of two additional Cypriot cylinder seals at nearby Tell Abu Hawam. The first excavator of the site—R. W. Hamilton—assigned them to Strata V and IV, that is, to the late phase of the Late Bronze Age and Iron Age I, but since both were found in an unclear context, it seems they represent additional Cypriot-Sea People remains at this site (Hamilton 1935:Nos. 217 and 245).

Like all the cultic objects discussed above, these cylinder seals also originated in Cyprus and their main period of distribution—in both Cyprus and Palestine— was the Late Bronze Age, with only a few continu-

ing into the early Iron Age. A. Mazar, who studied the Cypriot cylinder seals of this period in Palestine, also noted that most of them belong to the Cypriot "common style" type, according to the terminology of E. Porada (1948). As in the seal from Dor, the figures of this group are depicted in a typical schematic manner; most of them human figures often standing with one or two outstretched hands, and large daggers and background motifs between them: Animals, heads of bulls, calves, or a tree. Mazar also noted:

> Some of the seals in this style found in Israel differ in their style from the seals from Cyprus or other sites in Syria and it is possible that they attest to a special production center connected with Palestine. Thus, for example, seal No. 217 from Tell Abu Hawam has no real parallel among the Cypriot finds and it is possible that it is one of the creations of artisans from Cyprus who settled in Palestine. (A. Mazar 1978:13-14)

In summary, the cylinder seal from Tel Dor (and perhaps also the two seals from Tell Abu Hawam) is without doubt of Cypriot origin and it was known on the island throughout the entire twelfth century BCE. In our opinion, it should be considered a cult object of the Sea Peoples, since in the periods in Palestine under discussion, cylinder seals were not employed for sealing, but were often deposited in temples as jewelry and dedicatory offerings. This practice commenced as early as the Late Bronze Age, probably because of the cult scenes depicted on them (as, for example, in the temples of Lachish, Tel Mevorakh, Beth-Shean and Hazor; and see Stern 1984:25), and continued into the Iron Age I.

Due to the almost complete absence of written material at the settlements of the Sea Peoples in the south or the north of the country, it cannot be assumed that this cylinder seal was intended for sealing any type of document, but it was probably imported, or produced in Palestine, as an article of jewelry to serve as a ritual of-

Figure 56. Cypriot cylinder seal from Dor.

fering, perhaps for the temple of the Sea Peoples at Dor, which was erected at the end of the twelfth or during the eleventh century BCE. A similar use may be ascribed to the two Cypriot cylinder seals from Tell Abu Hawam.

*   *   *

It seems now to me that if we sum up the present evidence as clearly indicated in the above discussion, the ten types of cult objects, many of them uncovered at Dor, share a number of common characteristics:

1. Almost all these cult objects had their source in Cyprus, but were locally produced in Palestine during the Iron Age I.

2. In the southern part of the country they are typical of the Philistine sites and strata.

3. Very small differences exist between the cult objects of the southern and those of the Northern Sea Peoples.

4. All these cult objects were intended to be used only by the Sea Peoples because they were part of their unique cult.

5
BURIAL PRACTICES

POTTERY BATH

The anthropoid clay coffins found at Beth-Shean (Rowe 1930: Pls. 37–40) will not be considered here for two reasons: They were discovered outside the area under discussion, and furthermore, they have been exhaustively studied by Trude Dothan and Eliezer Oren, who differ in their views, and others (T. Dothan 1982:252–288; Oren 1973:101–153), and there does not seem to be anything new that can be added to the subject.

We do wish, however, to call attention to a particularly important pottery "bath" found in Stratum VI at Megiddo (Harrison 2004:Pl. 21.1, here Fig. 57). A. Mazar reopened discussion of this object in his review of Harrison's study and in our opinion he has correctly defined its context. According to Mazar:

> The pottery "bath" was compared by Harrison with Mesopotamian examples, yet as the author mentions, such Mesopotamian examples are unknown in the Levant before the Assyrian conquest. A more relevant reference would be Karageorghis (2000:266–274), who discusses the Megiddo example as well as several other pottery and stone bathtubs from Philistia in relation to contemporary or somewhat earlier examples from Cyprus and the Aegean. The bath from Megiddo should be seen in this context: As some of the items at Megiddo VI that might be related to "Sea Peoples and Aegean / Cypriot connections. (Mazar 2007:84)

In addition to Mazar's conclusion, it should also be mentioned that the bath [coffin] continued an earlier tradition of clay coffins of Aegean origin uncovered in Palestine from the Late Bronze Age, like the coffin found north of 'Akko (Ben-Arieh-Edelstein 1977: 9, Pl. XV:10).

It seems to the present writer that some pottery sherds from one of the Philistine strata at Ashkelon shown to him by Daniel Master and not yet published also belong to a similar "bath."

Regarding the origin of the stone bathtub, of which an example was also found at Megiddo in Stratum VI (locus 1756) and published by Harrison (Harrison 2004: 239, Fig. 96), we can unfortunately shed no light (and cf. now Birney and Doak 2011 on Philistine burial customs and bibliography there).

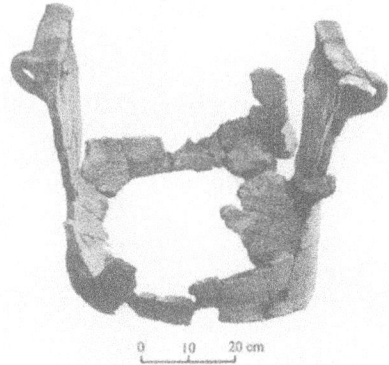

Figure 57. Pottery bath from Megiddo.

GOLD PLAQUES

Further proof of an Aegean burial custom may be found in three gold mouth-plaques (Harrison 2004:Pl. 28.2, 4–5) in cave 39 at Megiddo dating to the Early Iron Age contemporaneous with Stratum VI (Fig. 58).

They resemble the gold mouth-plaques found previously in one of the anthropoid coffins at Beth-Shean (Rowe 1930; Oren 1973:76:11, Pl. 39:2). These coffins are generally attributed to the Philistines since it is unknown as a local burial custom. Despite their paucity, the author considers these mouth plaques of special importance in providing evidence of the existence of the Northern Sea Peoples at Megiddo.

Figure 58. The gold plaques from Megiddo VIA.

6
VARIOUS TOOLS AND FINDS

BRONZE AXES AND KNIVES

We have described above the remains of the metallurgy industry of the Sea Peoples at Dor, 'Akko, Megiddo, Yokne'am, and elsewhere. Aside from the metal-processing residue, we also found several bronze tools which were probably manufactured at Dor: Two of these, a knife and the blade of a pick (Fig. 59), were discovered in Area G in situ in Stratum 10, the stratum of the Sikils, close to the extensive metal working area. These two bronze tools are not cult objects and have no special characteristics.

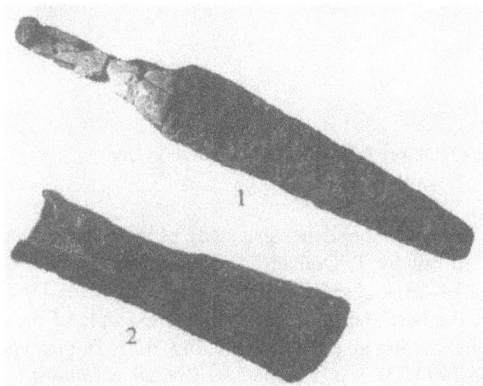

Figure 59. Knife (1) and bronze pick (2) from Area G at Dor.

Other bronze objects, on the other hand, which can be identified as weapons and connected with the Sea Peoples, were found at Tell Qasile and at Megiddo. In his review of Harrison's *Megiddo 3*, A. Mazar noted:

> The bronze objects from Megiddo VIA are described in detail, yet [Harrison] does not sufficiently emphasize the significance of several bronze objects with close parallels in the Aegean and in Cyprus, such as the double ax, adze axes, and shafted spear heads (Harrison 2004, pls. 31:7-10; 35:2-4, here Fig. 60). These objects, like others in Stratum VIA, are important for recognizing the non–Canaanite components in Stratum VIA. (A. Mazar 2007:84)

The present writer fully agrees with these observations.

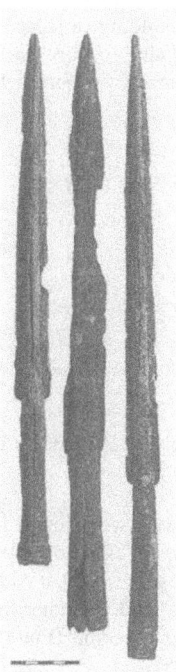

Figure 60. Shafted spear heads from Megiddo VIA.

Additional shafted spear heads similar to those of Megiddo VI had been found in Tell Qasile XI (Mazar 1985a:4, photo 2) and Tel Zeror (Ohata 1970: Pl. LXIII: 6-7), a site which has already been discussed as included in the territory of the Northern Sea Peoples. Others have been found at cist grave 1029 at Akhziv (Prausnitz 1997:22), which had been dated to the eleventh century BCE, and also in the Jatt hoard, where the source of these spears was discussed by M. Artzy (2006:60-61) who also dated them to the eleventh century BCE.

As to the double axes, at Tell Qasile, Mazar had found one bronze axe with a double blade (Fig. 61:3); it was described in the excavation report as follows:

> This object was found on the step leading to the raised platform of Temple 131 of Stratum X (eleventh century BCE). It is well preserved. The tool has two blades, perpendicular to one another. Metallurgical analysis revealed: Copper 88%, Tin 10%, Lead 1%, Silver 1%. The quantity of tin is indicative of the good quality of the bronze. (A. Mazsr 1985a:3-4, here, Fig. 61:3)

Close parallels from Israel, as mentioned above, come from Megiddo, Stratum VIA. Of four similar Megiddo tools (Harrison 2004, Pl. 31:7–10), two were found in the public building (a palace or temple), near the entrance to the city (one of them together with "Philistine" pottery and a wall bracket; see Figs. 50:4; 51 and 61:1–2).

stratum of a thick burnt layer (stratum 9) of ashes similar to that which sealed the Sikil layer in Area B1 (Stern 2000a:349; Matskevich 2003; here, Fig. 62:2).

The second bone-handle fragment of the same peculiar type was found in the 2000 season in Area D2 (not yet published), on the floor of the earliest Sikil structure built in this area just above the natural rock (Strata 13-12).

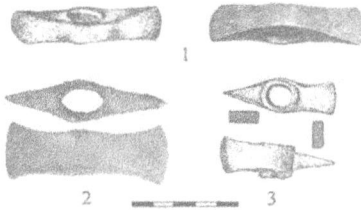

Figure 61. Bronze axes: 1-2: Megiddo; 3: Tell Qasile.

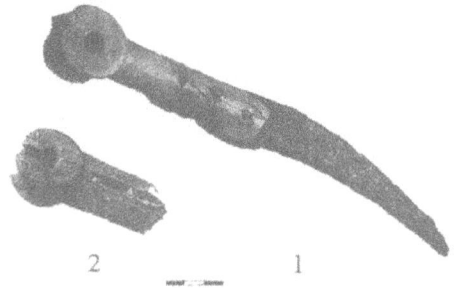

Figure 62. Ivory knife handles: 1: Ekron; 2: Dor.

Similar double axes were found in two additional sites in Israel, outside but close to the territory discussed here: One in the cist grave 1029 at Akhziv, dated to the eleventh century BCE, and the other in the hoard from Jatt, dated to the same period (Prausnitz 1997:22-23; Artzy 2006:60-62; 95).

Outside Israel the type is known in a wide geographical area and chronological range. The closest parallels to the Qasile and Megiddo axes are from Crete and Cyprus (cf. Catling 1964; Miron 1985; and cf. Artzy 2006:60-62).

The most comprehensive study of these knives was carried out by T. Dothan (T. Dothan 1989a:154–163; 2002:14–23; and see detailed bibliography there). Up to now, the best and the most complete example of these knives was found at Ekron (here, Fig. 62:1; Dothan and Gitin 1990:33). It is described by Dothan as follows:

IVORY KNIFE HANDLES

When describing the remains of the Sikils' metalworking at Dor, we have claimed that no evidence of an iron metallurgical industry had been uncovered there. All the metalworking seemed to belong to the regular manufacture of bronze tools. The only exceptions were two bone handles of cultic knives of which no remains of their metal blades were preserved. If we compare them with similar complete knives from the Philistine sanctuary at Ekron, perhaps they too possessed iron blades which were not necessarily produced at Dor.

In any case, the two knife handles, the shape of which is exclusive to the Sea Peoples in Palestine, were uncovered at Tel Dor, one of them in the southern part of Area G, within the upper Sikil

A complete iron knife with worked ivory handle and bronze rivets was found on the floor of building 350 room C. The ivory handle terminates in a ring-shaped pommel with a central suspension hole. The pommel is perpendicular to the axis of the blade, which is slightly curved and sharpened on its concave edge. Its tang is wider than the handle plate. Three bronze rivets, inserted longitudinally along the blade's axis, secure the blade to the handle. What appears to be the negative of caps encircle the rivet holes on the handle plate. The caps were not preserved, but may have been made of precious metal, such as gold (Karageorghis 1981:148–149, Pl. XXIV). The elegant craftsmanship of this knife and the context in which it was found clearly indicate a cultic or ceremonial function. The combination of different metals and materials in a single object for aesthetic effect indicates that these were luxury, rather than utilitarian, items (Waldbaum 1982: 328–329). The floor on which the knife was found was rich in pottery, predominantly of the Philistine Bichrome type. (T. Dothan 2002:14)

In addition to the complete knife, at least four similar handles were found in Ekron. Others were uncovered at other Philistine sites such as Tell Qasile. More came from northern sites such as Megiddo and Beth-Shean, to which the two from Dor can be added (Sherratt 1994; and cf. recently Mazar 2006:494-496).

T. Dothan attributes the origin of this knife-type to Cyprus, especially Enkomi, where many were found, but also other sites. However, there can be no doubt that the appearance of these small iron artifacts within the Sea People strata has an important bearing on the use of iron in the country (Muhly 1982; Muhly, Maddin, and Karageorghis 1982).

CYPRO-MINOAN INSCRIPTIONS

The only inscriptions for which an early Philistine script has been suggested are the Tell Deir Alla Tablets, two seals from Ashdod, and recently also the Tel Aphek fragment. We do not intend here to treat them; this has ably been done recently by I. Singer (Singer 2009; cf also Gadot 2006:27; Yasur-Landau 2002:413; Yasur-Landau and Goren 2004; Singer 1983). A later Philistine inscription from Tell eş-Şâfi/Gath was recently published by A. Maeir, who deals with the later development of the Philistine script (Maeir et al. 2008).

More concrete evidence is provided by an ostracon and jar handles inscribed in Cypro-Minoan script unearthed at Ashkelon and attributed by Cross and Stager to the Sea Peoples (Cross and Stager 2006:129–159, here Fig. 63).

It is significant that the majority of these jar handles (8 out of 12) were produced in the north of the country, in the area around 'Akko and one even in Dor. Cross and Stager describe the date and provenance of these vessels as follows:

> The ostracon and the other 12 inscribed handles, all from storage jars, or amphorae, were found in or near domestic quarters, dating from the twelfth–eleventh centuries BCE, near the center of the mound. Petrographic analysis shows that the ostracon originated in Ashkelon. Seven of the inscribed amphora handles were manufactured in coastal Lebanon, somewhere between 'Akko and Tyre; one (No. 6) in or near Dor; and one in or near Ashkelon. Two came from an unknown source, and one has not yet been analyzed by petrography for provenance. (Cross and Stager 2006:129)

On the basis of this evidence, it is very likely that those eight handles were inscribed by the Northern Sea Peoples living in the region.

Figure 63. Inscribed handle from Ashkelon.

In this matter we should perhaps add here the finds of the "Philistines seals," i.e., "anchor" seals considered by O. Keel and others as "Philistine" objects; and perhaps also some pyramidical seals as well (Keel 1994; Keel, Shuval, and Uhlinger 1999:72-76; Herzog in Stern 1993:484; Harrison 2003:102, Pl. 40:2). These seals have been found in most of the Philistine settlements in the south, but also in Tell Qasile and Tel Gerisa, and in the Northern Sea Peoples sites such as Megiddo (three—one of them in Stratum VIA), Tell Keisan (Stratum IXc), and 'Akko, all dated to the eleventh century BCE (Keel 1994; here Fig. 64). If they do belong to the Sea Peoples we may consider them to be used in sealing documents.

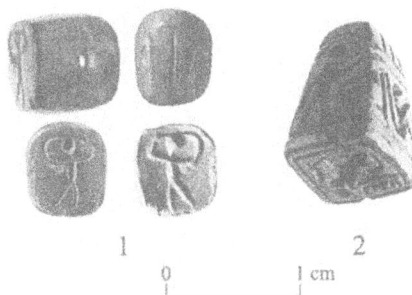

Figure 64. "Philistine" seals: 1. Megiddo IVA ; 2: Tel Gerisa.

CLAY LOOM WEIGHTS

Clay loom weights found in Palestine and attributed to the Sea Peoples are of two different types. The southern type has been found by the hundreds at Ashkelon and all other Philistine sites (Stager 1991:14–15; Cassuto 2012:470). The second type has been found at only three sites: Megiddo, Tell Keisan, and Tell Qasile; not a single one has been found south of the Yarkon River. According to L. E. Stager these loom weights, in both southern variety ("spoolweights") and the northern variety (pierced-cylinder weights), are in the Aegean tradition.

In Megiddo Stratum VIA were found many clay loom weights in building 2072 (the "palace") (Harrison 2004: 59–60, 196, Fig. 33, here Fig 65:1). They are compared by Harrison with clay spools of Aegean-type loom weights typical of the Philistine layer at Tel Miqne and Ashkelon. However, this parallel is not accurate except for one single weight from Megiddo (ibid, Pl. 21:2), which indeed recalls the southern Philistine "spoolweights." All the other weights from Megiddo VI are of the second pierced cylinderical weights type.

Many loom weights identical to those of Megiddo VI were found also in the excavations at Tell Qasile Stratum X (Shamir 1994, here Fig. 65:1-2). Shamir maintains that loom weights of this type are very rare and, aside from Megiddo and Tell Qasile, they are found only at Tell Keisan (Briend and Humbert 1980:315–321).

The discovery of such weights at Megiddo, Tell Keisan, and Tell Qasile should not be a surprise since, as we have pointed out above, we believe that the line of settlement along the Yarkon—Aphek, Tell Qasile, Tel Jerishe, and also Jaffa and its surroundings—served as the meeting point of the Northern Sea Peoples and the Philistines, and it should not be considered, as do Yuval Gadot and others, only as Philistia's "northern boundary line" (Gadot 2006). It therefore seems that the distribution of this type of loom weight is unique to the Northern Sea Peoples, as compared with the southern loom weights characteristic of the Philistines which appear only from Qasile southward (and see also recently: Rahmstorf 2003; 2005; Mazow 2006-07; Yasur-Landau 2009).

*   *   *

The examples of objects discussed above do not represent all the objects associated with the Northern Sea Peoples: We have not discussed, for example, the pottery kernoi, of which quite a few have been found at Megiddo VI (Harrison 2004:Pl. 23) and whose Philistine origin in Palestine has been studied extensively by T. Dothan (T. Dothan 1982:222–227). Other possible objects of pottery and bronze include the bird-headed bowl, examples of which were discovered at Philistine Ashdod and Qasile (T. Dothan 1982:228, Pls.9–10) and Megiddo VI (Zarzecki-Peleg 2005:Fig. 42:1), as well as "Cypriot" bronze artifacts (Artzy 2006) .

Figure 65. Northern Sea People loom weights: 1: Megiddo VIA; 2: Tell Qasile X; 3: Philistine loom weight from Megiddo VIA.

7
CONCLUSIONS

I will preface this section by repeating my three main conclusions presented in the introduction:

1. In the area examined it is possible to distinguish the material culture characteristic of the Northern Sea Peoples which exhibits elements that are partly identical with and partly unlike those of the Philistines.

2. The source of this culture is derived almost in its entirety from Cyprus but the great majority of the finds were manufactured in the northern Palestinian coast by local Sea Peoples and not imported through trade with Cyprus, for at that time many of them ceased to be produced in Cyprus itself.

3. The time range of this culture is of briefer duration than that of the Philistines and apparently did not last much longer than one hundred and thirty years: From the end of the twelfth century, or perhaps a little later, to the very end of the eleventh century, when it was displaced in its entirety by the local Israelite culture.

The reasons for these conclusions are as follows:

In the geographical area under study, namely, the coastal area of Palestine from the Yarkon northward, the 'Akko Plain, and the western Jezreel Valley, all the settlements containing strata from the end of the Late Bronze Age came to an end in a destruction that was attributed by almost all their excavators to the Sea Peoples.

Some of the destroyed settlements were never rebuilt (Tel Nami); others were rebuilt only after a gap during the twelve–eleventh centuries in the tenth century by Phoenicians and Israelites (Tel Michal and Tel Mevorakh). Some new settlements were established by the Sea Peoples on virgin soil (for example, Tell Qasile).

All the other settlements of the Sea Peoples (such as Tel Ḥefer, Tel Zeror, Tel Dor and Shiqmona) were rebuilt on the ruins of the earlier Canaanite sites; nearly all the excavators attribute this new construction and the different culture to the Sea Peoples.

The Northern Sea Peoples, who probably arrived in Palestine from Cyprus by boats (and cf. the naval depictions on the Carmel Coast and 'Akko, above Figs. 9 and 11), initially dwelled in the coastal cities, and later moved inland, similar to the movement of the Philistines several generations previously in the southern part of the country.

According to the evidence from Dor, the urban area was expanded by the new arrivals to five times the conjectured extent of the Canaanite city, and in some of its phases the new city was enclosed by a strong wall. Based on the finds from Dor, 'Akko, Megiddo and Yokne'am, the newcomers were partly engaged in the metalworking industry (bronze).

In all the settlements studied, a special type of monochrome pottery was distinguished in strata dating to the Iron Age I which, due to its shape or decoration, should be ascribed to the Northern Sea Peoples. Although this ware and other pottery objects of the Northern Sea Peoples were derived from Cyprus, they were not imports—all the petrographic tests conducted on this ware indicated that they were locally produced not by the Cypriot "Trading Diaspora" (Sherratt and Sherratt 1991:354) but—as I believe—by local residents of the Sea Peoples.

Indeed, the study of the material culture of the Northern Sea Peoples does not rely only on their distinctive pottery but also on the many other typical features of a population that has its own material culture. We have enumerated above several of these: Cult vessels produced in a variety of materials that include clay, ivory, metal, bone, and stone. Other evidence comes from everyday objects such as knives, axes, weapons, and loom weights, as well as funerary practices such as the pottery "bath" and the gold plaques, and possibly also vestiges of writing attributed to them. Regarding some of these objects, such as the lioness cups and cow scapulae, a strong resemblance can be noted between those ascribed to the Philistines and those of the Northern Sea Peoples; others are typical of the Northern Sea Peoples alone.

The occupation of the Sea Peoples in the north took place later than that of the Philistines, as is evidenced by the absence in the north of the early phase of the pottery corresponding to Mycenaean IIIC ware. Their occupation was contemporaneous with the bichrome stage of Philistine pottery and it can therefore be concluded that it was probably of shorter duration.

Most of the northern settlements established in this period were composed of two or more strata of which the earlier exhibits marked Cypriote and Canaanite influences, while the later stratum indicates the presence of three different influences: Indigenous Canaanite, Cypriot and the beginning of Phoenician influence (i.e., new Canaanite). Because of the appearance of bichrome Phoenician pottery in Stratum X at Tell Qasile. It is very likely that this site as well as the neighboring sites along the Yarkon such as Aphek, Jaffa, Tel Gerisa, and perhaps also Azor, were established in this time and flourished since they served as the "meeting places" of the two entities, and probably had a mixed population of both southern and Northern Sea Peoples.

For these reasons it becomes clear that the first wave of settlement of the Northern Sea Peoples was a large one which successfully seized control of the major cities in the north (cf. Wenamun and Dor), whereas in the later wave (or waves) of settlement, the population in these territories had became more heterogeneous.

At the end of the eleventh or the beginning of the tenth century BCE, all the above settlements were totally destroyed (from Tel Ḥefer to Tel Michal, Tel Mevorakh, Dor, Shiqmona, 'Akko, Tell Keisan, Tell Abu Hawam, Tel Qashish, Yokne'am, Tel Qiri, Megiddo and Afula; see above) and cities with an Israelite material culture replaced them. (cf. in this matter Halpern 2009).

Lastly, sometimes it is very difficult to identify the material culture of an ethnic element that spent only about hundred years in Palestine, but not in our case: For the impact of the Northern Sea Peoples in the territories in which they lived during this short period of time is most impressive.

BIBLIOGRAPHY

Aharoni, Y.
1958   Zephath (SFT) of Thutmose III. *Bulletin of the Israel Exploration Society* 22:138-39 (Hebrew).

Amiran, R.
1969   *Ancient Pottery of the Holy Land.* Jerusalem: Massada.

Arie, E.
2004   Intrasite Spatial Analysis in the Pottery of Megiddo VIA. Unpublished M.A. thesis, Tel Aviv University (Hebrew).

Arie, E.
2006   The Iron Age I Pottery: Levels K-5 and K-4 and Intrasite Spatial Analysis of the Pottery from St. VIA. Pp. 191-298 in *Megiddo IV: The 1998-2002 Seasons*, eds. I. Finkelstein, D. Ussishkin, and B. Halpern. Monograph Series of the Institute of Archaeology Tel Aviv University No. 24. Tel Aviv: Tel Aviv University.

Arie, E., Buzaglo, E., and Goren, Y.
2006   Petrographic Analysis of Iron I Pottery. Pp. 558-76 in *Megiddo IV: The 1998-2002 Seasons*, eds. I. Finkelstein, D. Ussishkin, and B. Halpern. Monograph Series of the Institute of Archaeology Tel Aviv University No. 24. Tel Aviv: Tel Aviv University.

Artzy, M.
1987   On Boats and Sea Peoples. *Bulletin of the American Schools of Oriental Research* 266:75-84.

Artzy, M.
1993   Tel Nami. Pp. 1095-98 in *The New Encyclopedia of Archaeological Excavations in the Holy Land*, ed. E. Stern. Jerusalem: Israel Exploration Society.

Artzy, M.
1995   Nami: A Second Millennium International Maritime Trading Center in the Mediterranean Pp. 14-71 in *Recent Excavations in Israel: A View to the West. Reports on Kabri, Nami, Miqne-Ekron, Dor, and Ashkelon*, ed. S. Gitin. Colloquia & Conference Papers 1. Dubuque, IA: Archaeological Institute of America.

Artzy, M.
2003   Mariners and Their Boats at the End of the Late Bronze and Beginning of the Iron Age in the Eastern Mediterranean. *Tel Aviv* 30:232-46.

Artzy, M.
2006   *The Jatt Metal Hoard in Northern Canaanite/Phoenician and Cypriot Context.* Cuadernos de Arqueología Mediterránea 14. Barcelona: Universidad Pompeu Fabra.

Åström, P.
1972   *The Late Cypriote Bronze Age, Architecture and Pottery.* Pp. 1-50. *The Swedish Cyprus Expedition, Vol. IV, Part IC.* Lund: Swedish Cyprus Expedition.

Bains, J.
1999   On Wenamun as a Literary Text. Pp. 209–33 in *Literatur und Politik im pharaonischen und ptolemäischen Ägypten: Vorträge der Tagung zum Gedenken an G. Posener, 5-10 September 1966 in Leipzig*, eds. J. Assmann and E. Blumenthal. Cairo: Institut Français d'Archéologie Orientale.

Balensi, J.
1980   Les fouilles de R. W. Hamilton à Tell Abu Hawam, Niveaux IV et V (1650–950 environs av. J.C.). Ph.D. dissertation, Université des Sciences Humaines. Strasbourg.

Balensi, J.
1981   Tell Keisan, Témoin original de l'apparition du "Mycénien III C 1a" au Proche-Orient. *Revue Biblique* 88:399-401.

Balensi, J.
1985   Revising Tell Abu Hawam. *Bulletin of the American Schools of Oriental Research* 257:65-74.

Balensi, J., and Herrera, M. D.
1985   Tell Abu Hawam 1983–1984, Rapport préliminaire. *Revue Biblique* 92:82-128.

Balensi, J., and Herrera, M. D.
1993   Tell Abu-Hawam. Pp. 10-14 in *The New Encyclopedia of Archaeological Excavations in the Holy Land*, ed. E. Stern. Jerusalem: Israel Exploration Society.

Barnett, R. D.
1975   The Sea Poeples. Pp. 359-78 in *Cambridge Ancient History, 3rd edition. Vol. 2/2.* Cambridge: Cambridge University Press.

Beck, P., and Kochavi, M.
1993   Aphek. Pp. 68-69 in *The New Encyclopedia of Archaeological Excavations in the Holy Land*, ed. E. Stern. Jerusalem: Israel Exploration Society.

Ben-Arieh, S., and Edelstein, G.
1977   Akko: Tombs near the Persian Garden. *'Atiqot* XII (English Series).

Ben-Dov, M.
1976   Napha—A Geographical Term of Possible 'Sea People' Origin. *Tel Aviv* 3:70-73.

Ben-Shlomo, D.
1999   Zoomorphic Terracottas of the Early Iron Age from Philistia. M.A. thesis, Hebrew University. Jerusalem (Hebrew).

Ben-Shlomo, D.
2008a   Zoomorphic Vessels from Tel Miqne–Ekron and the Different Styles of Philistine Pottery. *Israel Exploration Journal* 58:24-47.

Ben-Shlomo, D.
2008b   The Cemetery of Azor and Early Iron Age Burial Practices. *Levant* 40:29-54.

Ben-Shlomo, D., and Dothan, T.
2006   Ivories from Philistia: Filling the Iron Age I Gap. *Israel Exploration Journal* 56:1-38.

Ben-Shlomo, D., and Press, M. D.
2009   A Reexamination of Aegean–Style Figurines in the Light of New Evidence from Ashdod, Ashkelon, and Ekron. *Bulletin of the American Schools of Oriental Research* 353:39-74.

Ben-Tor, A.
1993   Jokneam. Pp. 805-11 in *The New Encyclopedia of Archaeological Excavations in the Holy Land*, ed. E. Stern. Jerusalem: Israel Exploration Society.

Ben-Tor, A., Bonfil, R., and Zuckerman, S.
2003   *Tel Qashish, A Village in the Jezreel Valley, Final Report*

of the Archaeological Excavations (1978–1987) Qedem Reports 5. Jerusalem: Institute of Archaeology, Hebrew University.

Ben-Tor, A., and Portugali, Y.
1987 *Tell Qiri: A Village in the Jezreel Valley.* Qedem 24. Jerusalem: Institute of Archaeology, Hebrew University.

Ben-Tor, A., Zarzecki-Peleg, A., and Cohen-Anidjar, S.
2005 *Yokne'am II, The Iron Age and the Persian Period.* Qedem Reports 6. Jerusalem: Institute of Archaeology, Hebrew University.

Bietak, M.
1993 The Sea Peoples and the End of the Egyptian Administration in Canaan. Pp. 292–306 in *Biblical Archaeology Today, 1990. Proceedings of the Second International Congress on Biblical Archaeology: Pre-Congress Symposium, Population, Production and Power, Jerusalem, June 1990.* Jerusalem: Israel Exploration Society.

Biran, A.
1994 *Biblical Dan.* Jerusalem: Israel Exploration Society.

Birney, K., and Doak, B. R.
2011 Funerary Iconography on an Infant Burial Jar from Ashkelon. *Israel Exploration Journal* 61:32-53.

Boaretto, E., et al.
2005 Dating the Iron Age I/II Transition in Israel: First Intercomparison Results. *Radiocarbon* 47:39-55.

Briend, J., and Humbert, J. B.
1980 *Tell Keisan : (1971-1976) : une cité phénicienne en Galilée.* Orbis biblicus et orientalis. Series archaeologica 1. Paris: J. Gabalda.

Brug, J. F.
1985 *A Literary and Archaeological Study of the Philistines* BAR International Series 265. Oxford.

Bunimovitz, S.
1990 Problems in the "Ethno" Identification of the Philistine Culture. *Tel Aviv* 17:210-22.

Burdajewicz, M.
1992 *Contribution au corpus céramique de Tell Keisan: Le niveau 13 augmenté du catalogue des importations chypriotes, mycéniennes, chypro-phéniciennes et de la céramique philistine.* Jerusalem: École Biblique et Archéologique.

Burdajewicz, M.
1994 *La céramique palestinienne du Fer I – La contribution de Tell Keisan, site de la Galilée maritime.* Ph.D. dissertation, Warsaw University. Warsaw

Cassuto, D.
2012 Weaving Implements. P. 470 in *Tell es Safi/Gath: The 1996-2005 Seasons*, ed. A. M. Maeir. Ägypten und Altestestament Band 69.

Catling, H. W.
1964 *Cypriot Bronze Work in the Mycenaean World.* Oxford: Clarendon Press.

Černý, J.
1952 *Paper and Books in Ancient Egypt, An Inaugural Lecture delivered at University College, London 29-May 1947.* London: H. K. Lewis.

Cohen-Weinberger, A., and Wolff, S. R.
2001 Production Centers of Collared-Rim Pithoi from Sites in the Carmel Coast and Ramat-Menashe Regions. Pp. 63-

657 in *Studies in the Archaeology of Israel and Neighboring Lands in Memory of D. L. Esse*, ed. S. R. Wolff. Studies in Ancient Oriental Civilization 59. Chicago-Atlanta: American Schools of Oriental Research.

Coubet, A.
1992 Reoccupation of the Syrian Coast after the Destruction of the "Crisis Years". Pp. 123–31 in *The Crisis Years: The Twelfth Century*, eds. W. A. Ward, and M. S. Joukowsky. Iowa: Kendall/Hunt Pub.

Cross, F. M., and Stager, L. E.
2006 Cypro-Minoan Inscriptions Found in Ashkelon. *Israel Exploration Journal* 56:129-56.

D'Agata, A. L., et al.
2005 Imported Pottery of LH IIIC style from Israel: Style, Provenance and Chronology. Pp. 371-79 in *Emporia. Aegeans in the Central and Eastern Mediterranean. Proceedings of the 10th International Aegean Conference, Athens, Italian School of Archaeology, 14-18 April 2004*, eds. R. Laffineur, and E. Greco. Liège: Université de Liège.

Dietrich, M., and Loretz, O.
1978 Das Seefahrende Volk von Sikilia. *Ugarit-Forschungen* 10:53-56.

Dothan, M.
1955 Excavations at 'Afula. *'Atiqot* I:18–63 (English Series).

Dothan, M.
1971 *Ashdod II-III: The Second and Third Seasons of Excavations 1963, 1965, Soundings in 1967.* 'Atiqot IX-X. Jerusalem.

Dothan, M.
1976 Akko: Interim Excavation Report First Season, 1973/4. *Bulletin of the American Schools of Oriental Research* 224:1-48.

Dothan, M.
1986 Sardinia in Akko? Pp. 105–15 in *Studies in Sardinian Archaeology. Vol. II: Sardinia in the Mediterranean*, ed. M. S. Balmuth. Ann Arbor: University of Michigan Press.

Dothan, M.
1989 Archaeological Evidence for Movements of the Early "Sea-Peoples" in Canaan. Pp. 59–70 in *Recent Excavations in Israel: Studies in Iron Age Archaeology*, eds. S. Gitin and W. G. Dever. Annual of the American Schools of Oriental Research 49. Winona Lake, IN: Eisenbrauns.

Dothan, M.
1993 Akko. Pp. 17–24 in *The New Encyclopedia of Archaeological Excavations in the Holy Land*, ed. E. Stern. Jerusalem - New York: Israel Exploration Society.

Dothan, M., and Ben-Shlomo, D.
2005 *Ashdod VI–The excavations of Areas H and K (1968-1969).* Israel Antiquities Authority Report 24. Jerusalem.

Dothan, M., and Freedman, D. N.
1967 *Ashdod I–The first season of excavations 1962.* 'Atiqot 7. Jerusalem.

Dothan, M., and Porath, Y.
1982 *Ashdod IV: Excavation of Area M. The Fortifications of the Lower City.* 'Atiqot 15. Jerusalem.

Dothan, T.
1982 *The Philistines and Their Material Culture* New Haven: Yale University Press.

Dothan, T.
1989a   Iron Knives from Tel Miqne-Ekron. *Eretz–Israel* 20:
         154–63 (Hebrew).
Dothan, T.
1989b   The Arrival of the Sea Peoples: Cultural Diversity in Ear-
         ly Iron Age Canaan. *The Annual of the American Schools
         of Oriental Research* 49:1–15.
Dothan, T.
1998   An Early Phoenician Cache from Ekron. Pp. 259-72 in
         Hesed Ve-Emet: Studies in Honor of Ernest S. Frerichs,
         eds. J. Magness and S. Gitin. Brown Judaic Studies 320.
         Atlanta:
Dothan, T.
2000   Reflections on the Initial Phase of Philistine Settlement.
         Pp. 145–48 in *The Sea Peoples and Their World: A Re-
         assessment*, ed. E. D. Oren. University Museum Mono-
         graph 108, University Museum Symposium Series 11.
         Philadelphia:
Dothan, T.
2002   Bronze and Iron Objects with Cultic Connotations from
         Philistine Temple Building 350 at Ekron. *Israel Explora-
         tion Journal* 52:1-27.
Dothan, T.
2003a   Ear Plugs from Ekron, Philistine Fashion. *Biblical Ar-
         chaeology Review* 29:46-64.
Dothan, T.
2003b   The Aegean and the Orient: Cultic Interaction. Pp. 189-
         213 in *Symbiosis, Symbolism, and the Power of the
         Past*, eds. W. G. Dever and S. Gitin. Winona Lake, IN:
         Eisenbrauns.
Dothan, T.
2006   A Decorated Ivory Lid from Tel Miqne – Ekron. Pp. 33-
         40 in *Confronting the Past: Archaeological and Histori-
         cal Essays on Ancient Israel in Honor of William. G. De-
         ver*, eds. S. Gitin, J. E. Wright, and J. P. Dessel. Winona
         Lake, IN: Eisenbrauns.
Dothan, T., and Dothan, M.
1992   *People of the Sea: The Search for the Philistines.* New
         York - Toronto: Macmilian Publishing Company.
Dothan, T., and Drenka, A. S.
2009   Incised Scapulae from a Cultic Assemblage at Philistine
         Ekron. *Eretz Israel* 29:105-14 (Hebrew).
Dothan, T., and Gitin, S.
1990   Ekron of the Philistines. *Biblical Archaeology Review* 16:
         20-36.
Dothan, T., and Gitin, S.
1994   Ekron of the Philistines. *Qadmoniot* 105-106:13-14 (He-
         brew).
Dothan, T., and Zukerman, A.
2004   A Preliminary Study of the Mycenaean IIIC:1 Pottery
         Assemblages from Tel Miqne-Ekron and Ashdod. *Bul-
         letin of the American Schools of Oriental Research* 333:
         1-54.
Egberts, A.
2001   Wenamun. Pp. 495-96 in *Oxford Encyclopedia of An-
         cient Egypt.* Vol. 3. Oxford: Oxford University Press.
Elgavish, J.
1994   *Shiqmona on the Seacoast of Mount Carmel.* Tel-Aviv:
         Hakibbutz Hameuchad Publ. House (Hebrew).

Fantalkin, A., and Yasur-Landau, A., eds.
2008   *Bene Israel: Studies in the Archaeology of Israel in Hon-
         our of Israel Finkelstein.* Leiden-Boston: Brill.
Finkelstein, I.
1995   The Archaeology of the United Monarchy–An Alternat-
         ive View. *Levant* 28:177-87.
Finkelstein, I.
1996   The Stratigraphy and Chronology of Megiddo and Beth-
         Shan in the 12th –11th Centuries BCE. *Tel Aviv* 23:170-84.
Finkelstein, I.
2000   The Philistine Settlement: When, Where and How Many.
         Pp. 159-80 in *The Sea Peoples and their World: A Re-
         assessment*, ed. E. D. Oren. University Museum Mono-
         graph 108, University Museum Symposium Series 11.
         Philadelphia: The University Museum, University of
         Pennsylvania.
Finkelstein, I.
2005   Megiddo 3: Final Report of the Stratum VI Excava-
         tions–A Review. *Biblical Archaeolgy Review* 31:64-66.
Finkelstein, I.
2006   The Last Labayu: King Saul and the Expansion of the
         First North Israelite Territorial Entity. Pp. 171- 87 in *Es-
         says on Ancient Israel in its Near Eastern Context: A
         Tribute to Nadav Na'aman*, eds. Y. Amit et al. Winona
         Lake, IN: Eisenbrauns.
Finkelstein, I.
2009   Destructions: Megiddo as a Case Study. Pp. 113-26 in
         *Exploring the Longue Durée: Essays in Honor of Law-
         rence E. Stager*, ed. J. D. Schloen. Winona Lake, IN:
         Eisenbrauns.
Finkelstein, I., and Piasetzky, E.
2008   Radiocarbon and the History of Copper Production at
         Khirbet en-Naḥas. *Tel Aviv* 35:82-95.
Finkelstein, I., and Piasetzky, E.
2009   Radiocarbon Date Destruction Layers: A Skeleton for
         Iron Age Chronology in the Levant. *Oxford Journal of
         Archaeology* 28:255-74.
Finkelstein, I., Ussishkin, D., and Halpern, B., eds.
2006   *Megiddo IV: The 1998-2002 Seasons.* Monograph Series
         of the Institute of Archaeology Tel Aviv University No.
         24. Tel Aviv: Emery and Claire Yass Publications in Ar-
         chaeology, Institute of Archaeology, Tel Aviv University.
Finkelstein, I., Zimhoni, O., and Kafri, A.
2000   The Iron Age Assemblages from Areas F, K and H and
         their Stratigraphic and Chronological Implications. Pp.
         244-324 in *Megiddo III*, eds. I. Finkelstein, D. Ussish-
         kin, and B. Halpern. Tel Aviv: Emery and Claire Yass
         Publications in Archaeology, Institute of Archaeology,
         Tel Aviv University.
Gadot, Y.
2006   Aphek in the Sharon and the Philistine Northern Border
         Frontier. *Bulletin of the American Schools of Oriental
         Research* 341:21-36.
Gadot, Y.
2008   Continuity and Change in the Late Bronze Age to Iron
         Age Transition in Israel's Coastal Plain: A Long Term
         Perspective. Pp. 55-73 in *Bene Israel: Studies in the
         Archaeology of Israel in Honour of Israel Finkelstein*,
         eds. A. Fantalkin and A. Yasur-Landau. Leiden-Boston:
         Brill.

Gadot, Y., and Yadin, E.
2009   *Aphek-Antipatris II–The Remains of the Acropolis.* Tel Aviv University, Monograph Series No. 27. Tel Aviv: Emery and Claire Yass Publications in Archaeology, Institute of Archaeology, Tel Aviv University.

Gardiner, A. H.
1947   *Ancient Egyptian Onomastica Vol. I.* Oxford: Oxford University Press.

Gilboa, A.
1999a   The View from the East–Tel Dor and the Earliest Cypro-Geometric Exports to the Levant. Pp. 119-39 in *Cyprus –The Historicity of the Geometric Horizon: Proceedings of an Archaeological Workshop, University of Cyprus, Nicosia, 11th October 1998*, eds. M. Iacovou and D. Michaëlidës. Nicosia Archaeological Research Unit, University of Cyprus.

Gilboa, A.
1999b   The Dynamics of Phoenician Bichrome Pottery. *Bulletin of the American Schools of Oriental Research* 316: 1-22.

Gilboa, A.
2001a   The Significance of Iron Age "Wavy –Band" Pithoi along the Syro-Palestinian Littoral, with Reference to Tel Dor Pithoi. Pp. 163-73 in *Studies in the Archaeology of Israel and Neighboring Lands in Memory of D. L. Esse*, ed. S. R. Wolff. Studies in Ancient Oriental Civilization 59; American Schools of Oriental Research Books 5. Chicago-Atlanta: American Schools of Oriental Research.

Gilboa, A.
2001b   Southern Phoenicia during Iron I-IIA in the Light of the Tel Dor Excavations: The Evidence of Pottery. Ph.D. dissertation, Hebrew University. Jerusalem.

Gilboa, A.
2005   Sea Peoples and Phoenicians along the Southern Phoenician Coast–A Reconciliation: An Interpretation of Sikila (SKL) Material Culture. *Bulletin of the American Schools of Oriental Research* 337:47-78.

Gilboa, A.
2006-2007   Fragmenting the Sea Peoples, with an Emphasis on Cyprus, Syria and Egypt: A Tel Dor Perspective. *Scripta Mediterranea* XXVII-XXVIII: 209-44.

Gilboa, A.
2009   Stratum VI at Megiddo and the "Northern Sea People Phenomenon". *Eretz-Israel* 29:82-91 (Hebrew).

Gilboa, A., Cohen-Weinberger, A., and Goren, Y.
2006   Philistine Bichrome Pottery–The View from the Northern Canaanite Coast: Notes on Provenience and Symbolic Properties. Pp. 303-34 in *Archaeological and Historical Studies in Honor of A. Mazar on the Occasion of his Sixtieth Birthday*, eds. A. Maeir and P. de Miroschedji. Winona Lake, IN: Eisenbrauns.

Gilboa, A., and Sharon, I.
2003   An Archaeological Contribution to the Early Iron Age Chronological Debate: Alternative Chronologies for Phoenicia and Their Effects on the Levant, Cyprus, and Greece. *Bulletin of the American Schools of Oriental Research* 332:7-80.

Gilboa, A., Sharon, I., and Zorn, J. R.
2004   Dor and the Iron Age Chronology: Scarabs, Ceramic Sequence and 14C Dating. *Tel Aviv* 31/1:32-59.

Gitin, S., Mazar, A., and Stern, E., eds.
1998   *Mediterranean Peoples in Transition: Thirteenth to Early Tenth Centuries BCE: In Honor of Professor Trude Dothan.* Jerusalem: Israel Exploration Society.

Gitin, S., Wright, J. E., and Dessel, J. P., eds.
2006   *Confronting the Past: Archaeological and Historical Essays on Ancient Israel in Honor of William G. Dever.* Winona Lake, IN: Eisenbrauns.

Goedicke, H.
1975   *The Report of Wenamun.* Baltimore: Johns Hopkins University Press.

Gunneweg, J., and Perlman, I.
1994   The Origin of Mycenaean IIIC:1 Stirrup Jar from Tell Keisan. *Revue Biblique* 101:559-561.

Guzowska, M., and Yasur-Landau, A.
2009   Anthropomorphic Figurines. Pp. 387-95 in *Aphek-Antipatris II, The Remains on the Acropolis. The Moshe Kochavi and Pirhiya Beck Excavations*, eds. Y. Gadot and E. Yadin. Tel Aviv University, Sonia and Marco Nadler Institute of Archaeology, Monograph Series 27. Tel Aviv: Institute of Archaeology, Tel Aviv University.

Halpern, B.
2009   The Dawn of an Age: Megiddo in the Iron Age I. Pp. 151-63. in *Exploring the Longue Durée: Essays in Honor of Lawrence E. Stager*, ed. J. D. Schloen. Winona Lake, IN: Eisenbrauns.

Hamilton, R. W.
1935   Excavations at Tell Abu-Hawam. *Quarterly of the Department of Antiquities in Palestine* 4/1-2:1-69.

Harrison, T. P.
2003   The Battleground (Who Destroyed Megiddo? Was It David or Shishak?). *Biblical Archaeology Review* 29: 30-35.

Harrison, T. P.
2004   *Megiddo 3: Final Report on the Stratum VI Excavations.* Oriental Institute Publications, Vol. 127. Chicago: The Oriental Institute of the University of Chicago.

Harrison, T. P.
2009   Lifting the Veil on a "Dark Age": Ta'yinat and the North Orontes Valley During the Early Iron Age. Pp. 171-84 in *Exploring the Longue Durée: Essays in Honor of Lawrence E. Stager*, ed. J. D. Schloen. Winona Lake, IN: Eisenbrauns.

Herzog, Z.
1993   Tel Gerisa. Pp. 480–84 in *The New Encyclopedia of Archaeological Excavations in the Holy Land*, ed. E. Stern. Jerusalem-New York.: Israel Exploration Society.

Herzog, Z., Rapp, G., and Negbi, O., eds.
1989   *Excavations at Tel Michal, Israel.* Monograph Series of the Institute of Archaeology of Tel Aviv University. No. 8. Minneapolis: University of Minnesota Press.

Humbert, J. B.
1981   Recents travaux à Tell Keisan (1979–1980). *Revue Biblique* 88:373-98.

Humbert, J. B.
1988   Tell Keisan entre mer et montagne. L'Archéologie entre texte et contexte. Pp. 65-83 in *Archéologie, art et histoire de la Palestine*, ed. E. M. Laperrousaz. Paris: Cerf.

Humbert, J. B.
1993   Tell Keisan. Pp. 862–67 in *The New Encyclopedia of Ar-*

chaeological Excavations in the Holy Land, ed. E. Stern. Jerusalem-New York: Israel Exploration Society.

Iacovou, M.
1992   Additions to the Corpus of the Eleventh Century BCE Pictorial Pottery. Pp. 217-26 in *Studies in Honor of Vassos Karageorghis*, ed. G. C. Ioannides. Nicosia: Society of Cypriot Studies.

Iacovou, M.
1994   The Topography of Eleventh Century BC Cyprus. Pp. 149–65 in *Cyprus in the 11th Century BCE*, ed. V. Karageorghis. Nicosia: University of Cyprus.

Iacovou, M.
1999   The Greek Exodus to Cyprus: The Antiquity of Hellenism. *Mediterranean Historical Review* 14:1-28.

Ilan, D.
1999   Northeastern Israel in the Iron Age I: Cultural, Socioeconomic and Political Perspectives. Ph.D. dissertation, Tel Aviv University. Tel Aviv.

Janeway, B.
2006-2007   The Nature and Extent of Aegean Contact at Tell Ta'yinat and Vicinity in the Early Iron Age: Evidence of the Sea Peoples? *Scripta Mediterranea* 27-28:123-46.

Kaplan, J., and Ritter-Kaplan, H.
1993   Jaffa. Pp. 655–59 in *The New Encyclopedia of Archaeological Excavations in the Holy Land*, ed. E. Stern. Jerusalem-New York: Israel Exploration Society.

Karageorghis, V.
1990   Miscellanea from Late Bronze Age Cyprus II. A Late Bronze Age Musical Instrument ? *Levant* 22:159.

Karageorghis, V.
1993   *The Coroplastic Art of Ancient Cyprus, Vol. 2: Late Geometric II and Cypro-Geometric III*. Nicosia: A.G. Leventis Foundation.

Karageorghis, V.
2000   Cultural Innovations in Cyprus Relating to the Sea Peoples. Pp. 255-79 in *The Sea Peoples and Their World: A Reassessment*, ed. E. D. Oren. University Museum Monograph 108, University Museum Symposium Series 11. Philadelphia: The University Museum, University of Pennsylvania.

Karageorghis, V., ed.
2001   *Defensive Settlements of the Aegean and the Eastern Mediterranean After c. 1200 B.C.* Nicosia: Trinity College Dublin.

Karageorghis, V., and Jacqueline
2006   A Propos des Appliqués Murales de Chypre. *Report of the Department of Antiquities, Cyprus* 2006:173-97.

Karageorghis, V., Picard, O., and Tytgat, C.
1987   *La nécropole d'Amathonte III: Tombes 113-367. The Terracottas; Statuettes, Sarchophages et Steles Decorees* Etudes Chypriotes IX. Nicosia: Department of Antiquities of Cyprus.

Keel, O.
1994   Philistine 'Anchor' Seals. *Israel Exploration Journal* 44: 21-35.

Keel, O., Shuval, M., and Uhlinger, C.
1990   *Studien zu den Stempelsiegeln aus Palästina/Israel. Band III: Die Frühe Eisenzeit: ein Workshop*. Freiburg–Göttingen: Vandenhoeck & Ruprecht.

Kelm, G. l., and Mazar, A.
1995   *Timna, A Biblical City in the Sorek Valley*. Winona Lake, IN: Eisenbrauns.

Kempinski, A.
1985   The Overlap of Cultures at the End of the Late Bronze Age and the Beginning of the Iron Age. *Eretz-Israel* 18: 399-407 (Hebrew).

Kempinski, A.
1989   *Megiddo, A City-State and Royal Centre in North Israel*. Munich: C.H. Beck.

Killebrew, A.
2000   Aegean Style Early Philistine Pottery in Canaan during the Iron I Age: A Stylistic Analysis in Mycenaean IIIC:Ib Pottery and its Associated Wares. Pp. 233-53 in *The Sea Peoples and their World: A Reassessment*, ed. E. D. Oren. University Museum Monograph 108, University Museum Symposium Series 11. Philadelphia: The University Museum, University of Pennsylvania.

King, P. J., and Stager, L. E.
2001   *Life in Biblical Israel*,. Louisville-London: Westminster John Knox Press.

Kingsleigh, S.
2000   Wenamun Docks at Dor. *Eretz-Israel* 29:70*-77*.

Kletter, R., Ziffer, I., and Zwickel, W.
2010   *Yavneh I. The Excavation of the 'Temple Hill' Repository Pit and the Cult Stands*. Orbis Biblicus Et Orientalis, Series Archaeologica 30. Fribourg: Vandenhoeck & Ruprecht GmbH.

Kochavi, M.
1989   *Aphek-Antipatris: 5000 Years of History*. Tel Aviv: Hakkibutz Hameuchad Publising House (Hebrew).

Kochavi, M.
1993   Tel Zeror. Pp. 1525-26 in *The New Encyclopedia of Archaeological Excavations in the Holy Land*, ed. E. Stern. Jerusalem-New York: Israel Exploration Society.

Koehl, R. B.
2006   *Aegean Bronze Age Rhyta*. Prehistory Monographs 19. Philadelphia: INSTAP Academic Press.

Lamon, R. S., and Shipton, G. M.
1939   *Megiddo I, Seasons of 1925-1934, Strata I-IV*. Chicago: University of Chicago.

Lehmann, G.
2001   Phoenicians in Western Galilee: First Results of an Archaeological Survey in the Hinterland of Akko. Pp. 65-112 in *Studies in the Archaeology of the Iron Age in Israel and Jordan, Journal for the Study of the Old Testament. Supplement Series; no. 331*, eds. A. Mazar and G. Mathias. Sheffield: Sheffield Academic Press.

Lehmann, G. A.
1979   Die Sikalaya. *Ugarit-Forschungen* 2:481-94.

Leonard, A., and Cline, E. H.
1988   The Aegean Pottery at Megiddo: An Appraisal and Reanalysis. *Bulletin of the American Schools of Oriental Research* 309:3-40.

Loud, G.
1948   *Megiddo II: Seasons of 1935-1939*. Chicago: University of Chicago Press.

Maeir, A.
2006   A Philistine "Head Cup" (Rhyton) from Tell es-Safi/

Gath. Pp. 335-34 in *"I Will Speak the Riddle of Ancient Times"- Archaeological and Historical Studies in Honor of Amihai Mazar on the Occasion of his Sixtiest Birthday*, eds. A. Maeir and P. de Miroschedji. Winona Lake, IN: Eisenbrauns.

Maeir, A.
2007   Ten Years of Excavations at Philistine Gath. *Qadmoniot* 133:15-24 (Hebrew).

Maeir, A., and Ehrlich, C. S.
2001   Excavating Philistine Gath. *Biblical Archaeology Review* 27:29.

Maeir, A., et al.
2008   A Late Iron Age I/Early Iron Age IIA Old Canaanite Inscription from Tell eṣ-Ṣâfi/Gath, Israel: Paleography, Dating, and Historical-Cultural Significance. *Bulletin of the American Schools of Oriental Research* 351:39-71.

Maisler, B.
1951   The Stratification of Tell Abu-Huwam on the Bay of Acre. *Bulletin of the American Schools of Oriental Research* 124:21-25.

Master, D. M.
2009   The Renewal of Trade at Iron Age I Ashkelon. *Eretz-Israel* 29:111*-122*.

Matskevich, S.
2003   The Early Iron Age at Tel Dor: An Analysis of the Stratigraphy and Pottery Assemblage of Area B1. M.A thesis, Hebrew University. Jerusalem (Hebrew).

May, H. G.
1935   *Material Remains of the Megiddo Cult*. Chicago: University of Chicago Press.

Mazar, A.
1978   Cylinder-Seals of the Middle and Late Bronze Ages in Eretz Israel *Qadmoniot* 41:6-14 (Hebrew).

Mazar, A.
1980   *Excavations at Tell Qasile, Part One: The Philistine Sanctuary Architecture and Cult Objects*. Qedem 12. Jerusalem: The Hebrew University of Jerusalem.

Mazar, A.
1985a   *Excavations at Tell Qasile, Part Two: The Philistine Sanctuary: Various Finds, the Pottery, Conclusions, Appendixes*, Qedem 20. Jerusalem: The Hebrew University of Jerusalem.

Mazar, A.
1985b   The Emergence of the Philistine Material Culture. *Israel Exploration Journal* 35:95-107.

Mazar, A.
1990   *Archaeology of the Land of the Bible: 10, 000-586 B.C.E.* Anchor Bible Reference Library. New York: Doubleday.

Mazar, A.
1993   Beth Shean in the Iron Age: Preliminary Report and Conclusions of the 1990–1991 Excavations. *Israel Exploration Journal* 43:201–29.

Mazar, A.
1994   The 11th Century BCE in the Land of Israel. Pp. 39–57 in *Cyprus in the 11th Century BCE*, ed. V. Karageorghis. Nicosia: University of Cyprus.

Mazar, A.
1997   Iron Age Chronology: A Reply to I. Finkelstein. *Levant* 29:157-67.

Mazar, A.
2000   The Temples and Cult of the Philistines. Pp. 213-32 in *The Sea Peoples and Their World: A Reassessment*, ed. E. D. Oren. University Museum Monograph 108, University Museum Symposium Series 11. Philadelphia: The University Museum, University of Pennsylvania.

Mazar, A.
2002   Megiddo in the Thirteenth–Eleventh Centuries BCE: A Review of Some Recent Studies. Pp. 264-82 in *Aharon Kempinski Memorial Volume: Studies in Archaeology and Related Disciplines*, eds. S. Ahituv and E. D. Oren. Beer-Sheva 15. Beer-sheva: Ben Gurion University of the Negev.

Mazar, A.
2005   The Debate over the Chronology of the Iron Age in the Southern Levant: Its History, the Current Situation, and a Suggested Resolution Pp. 15-30 in *The Bible and Radiocarbon Dating: Archaeology, Text and Science*, eds. T. E. Levy and T. Higman. London: Equinox.

Mazar, A.
2006   *Excavations at Tel Beth-Shean 1989-1996 Vol. I: From The Late Bronze Age IIB to the Medieval Period*. Jerusalem: Israel Exploration Society.

Mazar, A.
2007   Review of: T. R. Harrison, *Megiddo 3. Bulletin of the American Schools of Oriental Research* 345:83-87.

Mazar, A., and Bronk Ramsey, C.
2008   14C Dates and the Iron Age Chronology of Israel: A Response. *Radiocarbon* 50:159-80.

Mazar, B.
1974   The Philistines and the Rise of Israel and Tyre. *The Israel Academy of Sciences and Humanities Proceedings* 1/7: 1-22.

Mazow, L.
2006-2007 The Industrious Sea Peoples: The Evidence of Aegean-Style Textile Production in Cyprus and the Southern Levant. *Scripta Mediterranea* 27-28:291-321.

Miron, E.
1985   Axes and Adzes in Israel and its Surroundings. M. A. thesis, Tel Aviv University. Tel Aviv

Moers, G.
1995   Die Reiseerzählung des Wenamun. Pp. 912–21 in *Texte aus der Umwelt des Alten Testaments (TUAT) Band 3: Mythen und Epen III*, eds. E. Blumenthal et al. Gutersloh: Mohn

Möller, G.
1909   *Hieratische Lesestücke für den akademischen Gebrauch 2: Literarische Texte des Neuen Reiches*. Leipzig Hinrichs.

Mountjoy, P. A.
1999   *Regional Mycenaean Decorated Pottery*. Radhen: M. Leidorf.

Muhly, J. D.
1982   How Iron Technology Changed the Ancient World and Gave the Philistines a Military Edge. *Biblical Archaeology Review* 8:40-54.

Muhly, J. D.
1984   The Role of the Sea Peoples in Cyprus During the LC III Period. Pp. 39-55 in *Cyprus at the Close of the Late Bronze Age*, eds. V. Karageorghis, and J. D. Muhly. Nicosia: A.G. Leventis Foundation.

Muhly, J. D., Maddin, R., and Karageorghis, V.
1982   *Early Metallurgy in Cyprus, 4000–500 BCE*. Nicosia: Pierides Foundation.

Nahshoni, P.
2009   A Philistine Temple in the North-Western Negev. *Qadmoniot* 138:88-92 (Hebrew).

Negbi, O.
1991   Were There Sea Peoples in the Central Jordan Valley at the Transition from the Bronze Age to the Iron Age? *Tel Aviv* 18:205-43.

Nibbi, A.
1985   *Wenamun and Alashia Reconsidered*. Oxford: DE Publications.

Nibbi, A.
1996   The City of Dor and Wenamun. *Discussions in Egyptology* 35:77-95.

Nilsson, M. P.
1950   *The Minoan-Mycenaean Religion*. Acta Regiae Societatis Humaniorum Litterarum Lundensis, Vol. 9. Lund: Biblo & Tannen Publishers.

O'Connor, D.
2000   The Sea Peoples and Egyptian Sources. Pp. 85-101 in *The Sea Peoples and Their World: A Reassessment*, ed. E. D. Oren. University Museum Monograph 108, University Museum Symposium Series 11. Philadelphia: The University Museum, University of Pennsylvania.

Ohata, K.
1967   *Tel Zeror II. Preliminary Report of the Excavation Second Season 1965*. Tokyo: Society for Near Eastern Studies in Japan.

Ohata, K.
1970   *Tel Zeror III. Preliminary Report of the Excavation Third Season 1970*. Tokyo: Society for Near Eastern Studies in Japan.

Oren, E. D.
1973   *The Northern Cemetery of Beth-Shan*. Leiden: Brill.

Oren, E. D., ed.
2000   *The Sea Peoples and their World: A Reassessment*. University Museum Monograph 108, University Museum Symposium Series 11. Philadelphia: The University Museum, University of Pennsylvania.

Paley, S. M., and Porath, Y.
1993   Tel Hefer. Pp. 612–13 in *The New Encyclopedia of Archaeological Excavations in the Holy Land*, ed. E. Stern. Jerusalem-New York: Israel Exploration Society.

Panitz-Cohen, N.
2003   Cypriot Wall Brackets in the Hecht Museum Collection. *Michmanim* 17:15*– 21*.

Panitz-Cohen, N.
2006   Off the Wall–Wall Brackets and Cypriots in Iron Age I Israel. Pp. 613-36 in *"I Will Speak the Riddle of Ancient Times"– Archaeological and Historical Studies in Honor of Amihai Mazar on the Occasion of his Sixtiest Birthday*, eds. A. Maeir and P. de Miroschedji. Winona Lake, IN: Eisenbrauns.

Panitz-Cohen, N., and Mazar, A.
2006   *Timnah (Tel Batash) III–The Finds from the Second Millennium BCE*. Qedem 45. Jerusalem: The Hebrew University of Jerusalem.

Panitz-Cohen, N., and Mazar, A.
2009   *Excavations at Tel Beth-Shean 1986-1996 Vol III. The 13th -11th Century BCE Strata in Areas N and S*. Jerusalem: Israel Exploration Society.

Pieridou, A.G
1971   *Jewellery in the Cyprus Museum*. Picture book, Republic of Cyprus, Department of Antiquities; no. 5. Nicosia: Dept. of Antiquities.

Porada, E.
1948   The Cylinder Seals of the Late Cypriot Bronze Age. *American Journal of Archaeology* 52:178-98.

Prausnitz, M. W.
1997   The Stratigraphy and Ceramic Typology of Early Iron-Age Tombs at Akhziv. *Michmanim* 11:17-30 (Hebrew).

Press. M.D
2012   *Ashkelon 4: The Iron Age Figurines of Ashkelon and Philistia*, Winona Lake, IN:Eisenbrauns.

Pritchard, J. B.
1968   New Evidence on the Role of the Sea Peoples. Pp. 99-112 in *The Role of the Phoenicians in the Interaction of Mediterranean Civilisations: Papers Presented to the Archaeological Symposium at the American University of Beirut; March, 1967*. ed. W. A. Ward. Beirut: American University of Beirut.

Raban, A.
1982   *Archaeological Survey of Israel, Nahlal Map*. Jerusalem Israel Antiquities Authority (Hebrew).

Raban, A.
1987   The Harbor of the Sea Peoples at Dor. *Biblical Archeologist* 50:118-26.

Raban, A.
1988   The Constructive Maritime Role of the Sea Peoples in the Levant. Pp. 261–94 in *Society and Economy in the Eastern Mediterranean (c. 1500–1000 BCE)*, eds. M. Heltzer and E. Lipiński. Orientalia Lovaniensia Analecta 23. Leuven: Peeters.

Raban, A.
1991   The Philistines in the Western Jezreel Valley. *Bulletin of the American Schools of Oriental Research* 284:17–27.

Raban, A., and Stieglitz, R. R.
1991   The Sea Peoples and their Contribution to Civilization *Biblical Archaeology Review* 17:34-42.

Rahmstorf, L.
2003   Clay Spools from Tiryns and Other Contemporary Sites. An Indication of Foreign Influence in LH IIIC?. Pp. 397-415 in *The Periphery of the Mycenaean World. 2nd International Interdisciplinary Colloquium: 26-30 September, Lamia 1999*, eds. N. Kyparissi-Apostolika and M. Papakonstaninou. Athens: Ypourgeio Politismou.

Rahmstorf, L.
2005   Ethnicity and Changes in Weaving: Technology in Cyprus and the Eastern Mediterranean in the 12th Century BC. Pp. 143-69 in *Cyprus: Religion and Society. From the Late Bronze Age to the End of the Archaic Period. Proceeding of an International Symposium on Cypriot Archaeology, Erlangen, 23-24 July 2004*, eds. V. Karageorghis, H. Matthäus, and S. Rogge. Möhness Warnel: Bibliopolis.

Reese, D. S.
2002   On the Incised Cattle Scapulae from the East Mediterra-

nean and Near East. *Bonner Zoologische Beiträge* 50/3: 183-98.

Reese, D. S.
2009   On Incised Scapulae and Tridacna. *Eretz-Israel* 29: 188*–93*.

Rowe, A.
1930   *The Topography and History of Beth Shan*. Philadelphia: The University Press for the University of Pennsylvania Museum.

Sandars, N.K
1985   *The Sea Peoples: Warriors of the Ancient Mediterranean*. London: Thames & Hudson.

Sass, B.
2002   Wenamun and His Levant 1075 BC or 925 BC? *Egypt and the Levant* 12:247–55.

Scheepers, A.
1991   Anthroponymes et toponyms du récit d'Ounamon. Pp. 17-83 in *Phoenicia and the Bible: Proceedings of the Conference Held at the University of Leuven on the 15th and 16th of March 1990*, ed. E. Lipiński. Studia Phoenicia 11; Orientalia Lovaniensia Analecta 44. Leuven: Peeters.

Schipper, B.
2005   *Die Erzählung des Wenamun: Ein Literaturwerk im Spannungsfeld von Politik, Geschichte und Religion*. Orbis biblicus et orientalis 209. Freiburg: Vandenhoeck & Ruprecht.

Schlipphak, R.
2001   *Wandappliken der Spätbronze- und Eisenzeit im östlichen Mittelmeeraum, Abandlugen des Deutschen Palästina-Vereins*. Wiesbaden: Harrassowitz.

Schloen, J. D., ed.
2009   *Exploring the Longue Durée: Essays in Honor of Lawrence E. Stager*. Winona Lake, IN: Eisenbrauns.

Shamir, O.
1994   Loomweights from Tell Qasile. Pp. 35-42 in *Israel–People and Land: Eretz Israel Museum Year Book 7-8 (1990-1994)*. Tel Aviv: Eretz Israel Museum. (Hebrew).

Sherratt, A., and Sherratt, S.
1991   From Luxuries to Commodities: The Nature of Mediterranean Bronze-age Trading Systems in *Bronze Age Trade in the Mediterranean*, ed. N. H. Gale. Studies in Mediterranean Archaeology 90. Jonsered: Åströms.

Sherratt, E. S.
1998   "Sea Peoples" and the Economic Structure of the Late Second Millennium in the Eastern Mediterranean. Pp. 292–313 in *Mediterranean Peoples in Transition: Thirteenth to Early Tenth Centuries BCE: In Honor of Trude Dothan*, eds. S. Gitin, A. Mazar, and E. Stern. Jerusalem: Israel Exploration Society.

Sherratt, E. S.
2013   The Ceramic Phenomenon of the "Sea Peoples": An Overview. Pp. 619-643 in *The Philistines and Other "Sea Peoples" in Text and Archaeology*, eds. A. Killebrew and G. Lehmann. Atlanta: Society of Biblical Literature.

Singer, I.
1983   Inscription from Aphek. *Cathedra* 27:19-26.

Singer, I.
1988   The Origin of the Sea Peoples and their Settlements on the Coast of Canaan. Pp. 239-50 in *Society and Economy*

in the Eastern Mediterranean (c. 1500-1000 B.C), eds. M. Heltzer and E. Lipiński. Orientalia Lovaniensia Analecta 23. Leuven: Peeters.

Singer, I.
1994   Egyptians, Canaanites and Philistines in the Period of the Emergence of Israel, Pp. 282-338 in *From Nomadism to Monarchy: Archaeological and Historical Aspects of Early Israel*, eds. G. Finkielsztejn and N. Na'aman. Jerusalem: Yad Izhak Ben-Zvi.

Singer, I.
2009   A Fragmentary Text from Tel Aphek with Unknown Script. Pp. 403-14 in *Exploring the Longue Durée: Essays in Honor of Lawrence E. Stager*, ed. J. D. Schloen. Winona Lake, IN: Eisenbrauns.

Singer, I.
2012   The Philistines in the North and the Kingdom of Taita Pp. 451-71 in *The Ancient Near East in the 12th–10th Century BCE–Culture and History. Proceedings of the International Conference held in Haifa at the University of Haifa, 25 May 2010*, eds. G. Galil et al. Alter Orient und Altes Testament Band 392. Münster: Ugarit-Verlag.

Singer-Avitz, L.
2009   Carbon 14–The Solution to Dating David and Solomon? *Biblical Archaeology Review* 35/3:28-71.

Stager, L. E.
1991   *Ashkelon Discovered: Fron Canaanites and Philistines to Romans and Moslems*. Washington, D.C: Biblical Arcahaeological Society.

Stager, L. E.
1995   The Impact of the Sea Peoples in Canaan (1185–1050 BCE). Pp. 333–48 in *The Archaeology of Society in the Holy Land*, ed. T. E. Levy. London: Leicester University Press.

Stager, L. E.
2001   Ashkelon, Ancient City of the Sea. *National Geographic Magazine* 75:66-93.

Stager, L. E., Schloen, J. D., and Master, D. M.
2008   *Ashkelon I*. Winona Lake, IN: Eisenbrauns.

Stern, E.
1978   *Excavations at Tel Mevorakh (1973-1976), Part One: From the Iron Age to the Roman Period*. Qedem 9. Jerusalem: Institute of Archaeology, Hebrew University.

Stern, E.
1984   *Excavations at Tel Mevorakh (1973-1976), Part Two: The Bronze Age*. Qedem 18. Jerusalem: Institute of Archaeology, Hebrew University.

Stern, E.
1990   New Evidence from Dor for the First Appearance of the Phoenicians Along the Northern Coast of Israel. *Bulletin of the American Schools of Oriental Research* 279: 27-34.

Stern, E.
1991   Phoenicians, Sikils and Israelites in the Light of Recent Excavations at Dor. Pp. 85–94 in *Phoenicia and the Bible: Proceedings of the Conference Held at the University of Leuven on the 15th and 16th of March 1990*, ed. E. Lipiński. Studia Phoenicia 11; Orientalia Lovaniensia Analecta 44. Leuven: Peeters.

Stern, E., ed.
1993a   *The New Encyclopedia of Archaeological Excavations in*

the Holy Land. Jerusalem–New York: Israel Exploration Society.

Stern, E.
1993b   The Renewal of Trade in the Eastern Mediterranean in Iron Age I. Pp. 325–34 in *Biblical Archaeology Today 1990: Proceedings of the Second International Congress on Biblical Archaeology: Jerusalem, June–July 1990*, eds. A. Biran and J. Aviram. Jerusalem: Israel Exploration Society.

Stern, E.
2000a   *Dor, Ruler of the Seas: Nineteen Years of Excavations at the Israelite-Phoenician Harbor Town on the Carmel Coast*. Jerusalem: Israel Exploration Society.

Stern, E.
2000b   The Settlement of the Sea Peoples in Northern Israel,. Pp. 197-12 in *The Sea Peoples and Their World: A Reassessment*, ed. E. D. Oren. University Museum Monographs 108; University Museum Series 11. Philadelphia: The University Museum, University of Pennsylvania.

Stern, E.
2006   The Sea Peoples Cult in Philistia and Northern Israel. Pp. 385-98 in *"I Will Speak the Riddle of Ancient Times": Archaeological and Historical Studies in Honor of Amihai Mazar on the Occasion of his Sixtieth Birthday*, eds. A. Maeir and P. de Miroschedji. Winona Lake, IN: Eisenbrauns.

Stern, E., ed.
2008   *The New Encyclopedia of Archaeological Excavations in the Holy Land Vol. 5. Supplementary Volume*. Jerusalem-New York: Israel Exploration Society.

Tubb, J. N.
1988   The Role of the Sea Peoples in the Bronze Industry of Palestine and Transjordan in the Late Bronze–Early Iron Age Transition. Pp. 99-112 in *Bronze Working Centers of Western Asia*, ed. J. Curtis. London: Kegan Paul International.

Tubb, J. N.
2000   Sea-Peoples in the Jordan Valley. Pp. 181–96 in *The Sea Peoples and their World: A Reassessment*, ed. E. D. Oren. University Museum Monograph 108, University Museum Symposium Series 11. Philadelphia: The University Museum, University of Pennsylvania.

Ussishkin, D.
1995   The Destruction of Megiddo at the End of the Late Bronze Age and Its Historical Significance. *Tel Aviv* 22: 240-67.

Van Beek, G.
1993   Tell Jemmeh. P. 669 in *The New Encyclopedia of Archaeological Excavations in the Holy Land*, ed. E. Stern. Jerusalem–New York: Israel Exploration Society.

Wachsmann, S.
1981   The Ships of the Sea Peoples. *The International Journal of Nautical Archaeology and Underwater Exploration* 10:187-220.

Wachsmann, S.
1997   Were the Sea Peoples Mycenaeans? Evidence of Ship Iconography. Pp. 339–56 in *Res Maritime: Cyprus and the Eastern Mediterranean from Prehistory through the Roman Period*, eds. S. Swiny, R. L. Hohlfelder, and H.

W. Swiny. Atlanta: American Schools of Oriental Research.

Waldbaum, J. C.
1982   Bimetallic Objects from the Eastern Mediterranean and the Question of the Dissemination of Iron. Pp. 325-47 in *Early Metallurgy in Cyprus, 4000-500 BC*, eds. J. D. Muhly, R. Madin, and V. Karageorghis. Acta of the International Archaeological Symposium, Early Metallurgy in Cyprus, 4000-500 BC. Nicosia: Pierides Foundation.

Webb, J.
1985   The Incised Scapula. Pp. 317–28 in *Excavations at Kition V: The Pre-Phoenician Levels, Part II*, ed. V. Karageorghis. Nicosia: Department of Antiquities, Cyprus.

Wilson, J. A.
1955   The Journey of Wenamun to Phoenicia. Pp. 25-29 in *Ancient Near Eastern Texts Relating to the Old Testament*, ed. J. B. Pritchard. Princeton: Princeton University Press.

Wolff, S. R.
1998   An Iron Age I Site at En Hagit (Northern Ramat Menashe). Pp. 449–54 in *Mediterranean Peoples in Transition: Thirteenth to Early Tenth Centuries BCE: In Honor of Professor Trude Dothan*, eds. S. Gitin, A. Mazar, and E. Stern. Jerusalem: Israel Exploration Society.

Wolff, S. R., ed.
2001   *Studies in the Archaeology of Israel and Neighboring Lands in Memory of D. L. Esse*. Studies in Ancient Oriental Civilization 59 (ASOR Books 5). Chicago-Atlanta: ASOR.

Wolff, S. R.
forthcoming   *'En Hagit: A Middle Bronze Age III and Iron Age I Site in Northern Ramat Menashe*. Israel Antiquities Authority Report. Jerusalem.

Yadin, Y.
1968   "And Dan Why Did He Remain in Ships?". *Australian Journal of Biblical Archaeology* 1:9-23.

Yadin, Y.
1970   Megiddo of the Kings of Israel. *Biblical Archeologist* 33: 66-96.

Yannai, E.
2002   An Iron Age Burial Cave (no. 6) at Et-Tayiba, *'Atiqot* 43:29*-56* (Hebrew)

Yasur-Landau, A.
2002   Social Aspects of Aegean Settlement in the Southern Levant at the End of the 2nd Millennium BCE. Ph.D. dissertation, Tel Aviv University. Tel Aviv

Yasur-Landau, A.
2005   Old Wine in New Vessels: Intercultural Contact, Innovation and Aegean, Canaanite and Philistine Foodways. *Tel Aviv* 32:168-91.

Yasur-Landau, A.
2006   A Late Helladic IIIC-Style Stirrup Jar from Level K-5. Pp. 299-302 in *Megiddo IV*, eds. I. Finkelstein, D. Ussishkin, and B. Halpern. Tel Aviv: Emery and Claire Yass Publications in Archaeology, Institute of Archaeology, Tel Aviv University.

Yasur-Landau, A.
2009   Behavioral Patterns in Transition: Eleventh-Century BCE. Innovation in Domestic Textile Production. Pp.

507-15 in *Exploring the Longue Durée: Essays in Honor of Lawrence E. Stager*, ed. J. D. Schloen. Winona Lake, IN: Eisenbrauns.

Yasur-Landau, A., and Goren, Y.
2004   A Cypro–Minoan Potmark from Aphek. *Tel Aviv* 31:22-31.

Yon, M.
1994   Animaux symboliques dans la céramique chypriote du XIe s. Pp. 189–201 in *Proceedings of the International Symposium "Cyprus in the 11th Century BC"*, ed. V. Karageorghis. Nicosia: A.G. Leventis Foundation.

Zarzecki-Peleg, A.
1997   Hazor, Jokneam and Megiddo in the Tenth Century BCE. *Tel Aviv* 24: 258-88.

Zarzecki-Peleg, A.
1997   A Late Iron I Cave at Tel Yoqne'am. M.A. thesis, Hebrew University of Jerusalem. Jerusalem (Hebrew).

Zarzecki-Peleg, A.
2005   Tel Megiddo During the Iron I and IIA-IIB Ages–The Excavations of the Yadin Expedition. Unpublished Ph.D. dissertation, Hebrew University of Jerusalem. (Hebrew).

Zertal, A
2008   El-Ahwat, Pp. 1563-1565 in *The New Encyclopedia of Archaeological Excavations in the Holy Land, Vol. V*, ed.

E. Stern. Jerusalem: Israel Exploration Society

Zevulun, U.
1986-87   The Appearance of Headed Cups in Canaan. *Israel: People and Land* 4: 111-32; 12*-13* (Hebrew, English Summary).

Zevulun, U.
1987   A Canaanite Ram-Headed Cup. *Israel Exploration Journal* 37:88-104.

Ziffer, I., and Kletter, R.
2007   *In the Fields of the Philistines, Cult Furnishings from the Favissa of a Yavneh Temple (Exhibition Catalogue)*. Tel Aviv: Eretz Israel Museum.

Zorn, J. R.
2009   The Daily Grind at Tel Dor: A Trough and Basin from an Iron Age I Kitchen. *Eretz-Israel* 29:267*-80*.

Zorn, J. R., and Brill, R. H.
2007   Iron Age I Glass from Tel Dor, Israel. *Journal of Glass Studies* 49:256-58.

Zukerman, A., et al.
2007   A Bone of Contention? Iron Age IIA Notched Scapulae from Tell eş-Şâfi/Gath, Israel. *Bulletin of the American Schools of Oriental Research* 347:57-81.

Zuckerman, S.
2008   Fit for a (not-quite-so-great) King: A Faience Lion Headed Cup from Hazor. *Levant* 40:115-25.

www.ingramcontent.com/pod-product-compliance
Lightning Source LLC
Chambersburg PA
CBHW051426290326
41932CB00048B/3235